GENERAL SIR GEORGE DON

and the dawn of Gibraltarian identity

A biography

By Sam G Benady

Published in Gibraltar by Gibraltar Books, PO Box 816, Gibraltar.

ISBN.- 1 919657 17 0

Copyright: Sam G Benady, 2006

Typeset and printed by tipografia la nueva-Tarifa, S.C.A., c/ Arapiles
11A, 11380 Tarifa, Cádiz, Spain.

GENERAL SIR GEORGE DON

and the dawn of Gibraltarian identity

To Judy Chakraverty
whose enthusiasm for
Don was so infectious

«Je vous ferai du bien malgré vous»

(Don's remark to the people of Jersey whenever they
opposed his reforms)

CONTENTS

LIST OF ILLUSTRATIONS

Front Cover: Portrait of Sir George Don, presented by the Catholic inhabitants of Gibraltar to the Civil Hospital, 1815 (Photo: S Finlayson)
Back Cover: The Quarantine Brig off Gibraltar – the Southern Pillar of Hercules in the Distance. (Watercolour by PM Francis, 1827)

Between Pages 70 and 71:

INTRODUCTION

George Don was a general who won no great battles. His outstanding qualities were his humanity, his ability to get on with people, his great administrative ability and his almost infinite capacity for hard work. From his very earliest days in the Army, these qualities were recognised by his superior officers, and he was entrusted with the most difficult diplomatic missions. But what gained him the approval of his immediate superiors and the respect of those under him was never likely to propel him into the public eye. He has therefore never attracted the attention of biographers, and most of the details of his early life remain obscure. Indeed, as we shall see, the few recorded biographical details which we have are incorrect in many respects. Davies,[1] in *Fort Regent*, makes the bald statement that Don's life is well-documented, but apart from Sullivan's [2] brief memoir of Don's early years in Jersey, I have been unable to trace any attempt at a biography, apart from the short entry in the *Dictionary of National Biography* and his obituary in *The Gentleman's Magazine*,[3] both of which, as we shall see, are incorrect in many respects, although in the new Oxford DNB some of these errors have been corrected.

Don's military career spanned the War of American Independence, the French Revolution and the Napoleonic Wars. His first sight of action was in Minorca, where he formed part of the heroic garrison which eventually had to yield Fort St Philip to the Spanish forces led by the Duc de Crillon. During the long years of conflict with revolutionary France, he took part in three campaigns in the Low Countries and Germany, none of which could be called an outstanding success. For his final command in active service, he was called again to the Low Countries, to take charge of the expeditionary force to the island of Walcheren, and to organise the safe withdrawal of the troops: not that he was expected to turn the tide of battle there, for it was far too late for that, but the authorities knew by now that if anyone could salvage anything from that debâcle, and preserve and repatriate as much of the invading force as possible, it was George Don. His victories were in times of peace, and when

1

the last of the wars against the French was all but over, he began what was to be perhaps the most productive period of his life, as Lieutenant Governor of Gibraltar.

From 1806 to 1831 - the last twenty five years of his life - he took up what was in effect a new career. With only two short breaks - the first was the ill-fated Walcheren expedition of 1809, and the second was his temporary retirement from his work in Gibraltar, from 1821 to 1825, when the Earl of Chatham, uncharacteristically, took over as 'hands on' Governor of Gibraltar - he was effectively the ruler of two widely different communities, Jersey and Gibraltar. The first three years of his Lieutenant Governorship of Jersey have been recorded by Sullivan (1885) but the projected second volume, which was to deal with the years 1810 to 1814, was never published.

There has up to the present been no detailed account written of his work during the long period (1814-31) during which he was Lieutenant Governor of Gibraltar. Historians of the Rock have only paid cursory tribute to one or other of his achievements. Sir William Jackson[4] devotes several pages to enumerating some of the improvements he initiated, and Dr John Hennen,[5] who was his contemporary in Gibraltar, records many of the improvements to the public health of Gibraltar which Don instituted; but no author has dealt comprehensively with what was in effect the rebuilding of a town and the forging of a community.

During Don's long period in office, Gibraltar was transformed from a run-down, dangerously polluted and ruinous garrison into a town which, by nineteenth century standards at least, must have been a pleasant and prosperous place to live in, populated by a people who despite their diverse origins were probably beginning to think of themselves as Gibraltarians. George Don must receive much of the credit for this embryonic sense of community, which arose at least partly as a result of his efforts during his time as Lieutenant Governor. Many other factors must have played their part, as will be discussed later on, but the central, dominating figure in this transition was the benign presence of George Don, whose seventeen year tenure as Lieutenant Governor is unprecedented in

Gibraltar's history, both in its length and in the benefits it conferred on the Rock and its people.

I am a Gibraltarian, and I am conscious that much of this biography is orientated towards Gibraltar. My interest in Don arose while I was researching the medical history of Gibraltar,[6] and because the material which was most accessible to me resides in that invaluable resource, the Gibraltar Government Archives, the most detailed section of this attempt at a biography deals with the period 1814 to 1831, when George Don was Lieutenant Governor of Gibraltar. This may disappoint those who would like to know more about his earlier career, as it certainly disappoints me, and I would be more than grateful for any additional information, especially about Don's private life, which would enable me to add more detail to the earlier part of this account.

NOTES

1. Davies. p 24
2. Sullivan, *passim*.
3. *Dictionary of National Biography*. OUP, 1885; *The Gentleman's Magazine*, March 1832, pp. 272-273..
4. Jackson. pp. 226ff.
5. Hennen. pp. 81 ff..
6. Benady, S. Chapter 3.

ACKNOWLEDGMENTS

I acknowledge with gratitude the generous financial support of the Gibraltar Government, through the Heritage Ministry, which has facilitated the publication of this work.

It would be impossible to list the many friends from all around the world who have helped me in this work, with encouragement and nuggets of information. Those on whom I relied most frequently for help are

Gibraltar: Tom Finlayson, Dennis Beiso (Gibraltar Government Archives); Jon Searle, Lorna Swift (Gibraltar Garrison Library); Tito Benady.

Jersey: Mary Billot, Librarian, Société Jersiaise; Catherine Burke, Archivist, Jersey Archives Service; Louise Downey, Curator of Art, Jersey Museums Service.

Scotland: CJ Burnett, Stephen Wood (Scottish United Services Museum, Edinburgh). Stephen Aynscough, custodian of the Anderson Collection, and great great great great great great nephew of Sir George Don.

To them, and to the many others who encouraged me to write this book, go my sincere thanks.

Chapter 1

EARLY DAYS AND MINORCA

George Don was born in Edinburgh on April 30th 1756. He was the second son of John Don, Esq, of that city.[1] His mother was Ann Seton, whose brother James later became Governor of the island of St. Vincent in the Caribbean.[2] His much older brother, William, who was nineteen when George was born, joined the Royal Navy, becoming a lieutenant in 1758, and commander in 1782, and rose to the rank of captain in 1809. William does not appear to have played a prominent part in any of the many naval battles of the Napoleonic Wars, and died in Whitehaven in 1816. John, his younger brother, eventually became a merchant in Jamaica.[3] One sister, Peggy, married Sir Thomas Hay of Alderston, and two others remained single.[4]

The Don family came from south-eastern Scotland, and George Don's great grandfather, William, had arrived in Edinburgh from Kelso in about 1700. He became a vintner, taking over the business of one John Mitchell, whose employee he had been, and marrying his widow. Later on the family, by now well to do, built a row of tenements, which were known for many years as 'Don's Close,' and was situated on the north side of Edinburgh's High Street.[5]

The *Dictionary of National Biography*, presumably following Don's obituary in *The Gentleman's Magazine*, states that George Don was the younger son of Sir Alexander Don of Newtondon, Berwickshire, and other authors, including Balleine, in his *Biographical Dictionary of Jersey*,[6] have assumed that this was correct; but in fact, Sir Alexander had only one son, also called Alexander, who inherited the baronetcy. George Don may indeed have been related to this family in some way: his grandfather came from Kelso, the nearest town to Newtondon, as did the first Alexander Don, who bought the property of Newtondon. When George and his two brothers jointly applied for a Charter of Arms in 1810, the arms they chose were remarkably similar to those of the Dons of Newtondon.[7]

George Don joined the Army in 1770 as an ensign in the 51st Foot, which was then stationed in Minorca. John Don senior must have prospered as a vintner in order to be able to afford to buy commissions for two of the three sons. Certainly, George Don appears to have been financially well off - he was always very generous and free-handed towards the many charitable causes which he espoused. However, his good financial status was probably not due to his own family's money - he was his elder brother William's main legatee, but William did not leave a large estate - but may have been the result of money inherited by his future wife from her father, Patrick, 5th Lord Elibank, who settled £5000 on the couple on their marriage; her uncle, General Murray, who was generous to his legitimate nephews in his Will, did not leave anything to his brother's illegitimate issue.

Don was promoted to Lieutenant in 1774. General Johnstone, who was Lieutenant Governor and Commander in Chief of the island at the time, must have detected in him the qualities of hard work, humanity and organisational capacity which were to serve the communities of Jersey and Gibraltar so well in the distant future, because he appointed the young Don to be his aide-de-camp. General Johnstone's successor, Lieutenant General the Hon James Murray, not only kept him on as his aide-de-camp when he became Governor in 1778, but also made him his military secretary.

General Murray was the fifth son of the 4th Lord Elibank. He was born about 1719, and had had a distinguished military career in Europe and America. He was with Wolfe at Quebec, and commanded the left wing of the army at the battle of the Plain of Abraham, where Wolfe fell. He was left in charge of Quebec, which he defended against the French in spite of being outnumbered. He was later made Governor of Quebec in 1760, a post which he occupied until 1766.

It was in Minorca that Don met Maria Margaretta Murray, General Murray's niece, who was later to become his wife and devoted companion for nearly fifty years. General Murray arrived

6

in Minorca on being appointed Lieutenant Governor in 1775. His ailing wife, Cordelia, who had to be lowered into a boat blindfold during a severe storm between Marseilles and Minorca, arrived in Minorca with Maria, who had apparently come out with the Murrays as Mrs Murray's companion.

Maria Murray is referred to by one author as General Murray's daughter,[8] but this is clearly a mistake; in her marriage contract [9] she is described as the daughter of Patrick, 5th Lord Elibank (General Murray's elder brother), who died in 1778 and had 'disposed of a large part of his property among his illegitimate children.' [10] However, Lady Elibank (who was herself called Maria Margaretta) had died much earlier (in 1762) without issue, and Patrick had not remarried; so young Maria Margaretta Murray, who was probably born at about this time, must have been illegitimate, although in that case it seems rather unusual that Lord Elibank should have chosen to name her after his deceased wife. However, Lady Elibank was known to have been tolerant of her husband's infidelities, and was kind to his natural children.[11]

Romance may have blossomed then between George and Maria, but they were soon to be parted. The North American colonists had rebelled against Britain; they were supported by France, but Charles III of Spain appeared to sit on the fence at first - he was, after all, a despot and could have had little sympathy for colonial rebels; in addition, he was piqued with France, which had not consulted him, as she was obliged to do by treaty, before going to war. He offered to mediate, but he was in fact preparing for war at the same time: he was not going to miss an opportunity to recapture Minorca and Gibraltar from the British. Spain declared war on Britain in June 1779, and immediately laid siege to Gibraltar. Minorca was sure to be assaulted soon by the French and Spanish armies under the Duc de Crillon, a Frenchman in the service of the King of Spain.

Murray had been busy reinforcing the defences of the citadel of Fort St. Philip, the only defensible stronghold in Minorca, since 1775, but it was poorly garrisoned with, by 1779, only 1400 effectives, the garrison having been depleted by fever. In addition, General

Eliott, the Governor of Gibraltar, where the blockade by Spanish and French forces had just started, had retained a battalion of the 71st Regiment, which had been destined to Minorca, for the defence of the Rock, an action which may have saved Gibraltar, but which deprived Murray of desperately needed reinforcements.

General Murray's wife, together with her companion and niece, Maria Murray, took ship for England. Mrs Murray, who had been ailing for some time, died shortly afterwards in Sussex, where her family came from – her father was a lawyer who had been Mayor of Hastings - in February 1779. Four years were to pass before Maria and George were to meet again.[12]

General Murray wasted no time in finding a second wife. He married the daughter of Mr Whitham, the British consul in Mallorca. Captain Abraham Whitham, who was ADC to General Eliott at Gibraltar, and who played a distinguished part in the Great Siege, was thus his brother in law. The second Mrs Murray was delivered of her first child, a daughter, in March 1781, and a few months later, again pregnant, she was packed off with the baby to Leghorn well before the siege of Fort St. Phillip began. General Murray had named the baby Cordelia, after the first Mrs Murray - an interesting parallel with Maria Margaretta Murray. Perhaps it was a family custom to name a daughter - whether legitimate or illegitimate - after a deceased wife.

Although the assault on Gibraltar began as soon as Spain declared war, Minorca was left alone for over two years. In the interim, the island served as an invaluable source of supplies and news for the beleaguered Rock. In letters from General Eliott in Gibraltar to General Murray,[13] Eliott commends Don to Murray for his efficiency in carrying out his requests for provisions.

In August 1781, the assault on Minorca finally began. On the 19th, Spanish troops were disembarked, and three hours later the whole island, including the town of Mahon, had been seized, and the British garrison prepared to defend themselves in the almost impregnable fortress of St Philip. Murray was confident that he could withstand a siege. There was no question of a blockade such as Gibraltar suffered because Fort St. Philip controlled the harbour, so that the arrival of supplies and reinforcements could not be prevented. These reinforcements included a force of Corsican volunteers, commanded by a nephew of the famous Corsican patriot Paoli.

In September, Don's clerk, John la Rivière, was offered a bribe by the Spanish commander to betray the garrison. He refused indignantly, but did not report the incident, fearing for the safety of his family, who lived in Mahon. On the 15th October, Captain George Don, who was now Adjutant General and also General Murray's private secretary, was sent by Murray to the Spanish commander, the Duc de Crillon, with a letter.

Don's report to Murray describes the encounter in his own words, which throw some light on his character. He tells how he was conducted to the Duke's private office by the Count de Crillon, the Duke's son:

> A little after the Count had retired the Duke locked the door of the room and asked me if Mr. La Rivière had communicated anything particular to me or my General.... My answer was in the negative regarding myself, and that I did not believe that he had acquainted General Murray of anything extraordinary. The Duke said he had only thrown out general hints to that gentleman of what he would hereafter communicate to me.... I then told the Duke that he need not be under the smallest uneasiness about anything which he had communicated to Mr. La Rivière, as I knew him to be a young man of great honour and integrity.... The Duke then said, I perceive, Sir, by General Murray's letter, that you are his relation,[14] and I understand you are his confidant, I shall therefore openly declare to you that I am authorised to treat with General Murray. If you choose it, Sir, I will show you the minister's letter; in short, your General may have whatever sum he pleases and one million at first. I then interrupted him, and told him it was unnecessary to proceed any further on that subject, and that both the minister and him were egregiously deceived in the character of General Murray. His Grace said he was charged with the negotiation of the affair, that he was confidently informed that General Murray had a strong party against him at Court, that he was ill-treated by some people at home, and that he might expect soon to be relieved [of his command?]. I told him, on the contrary, tho' he might have

some enemies, I believed he was very well at Court, and imagined his Grace to be misinformed. The Duke said that the fiscal, Don Peter Surtas, had been intercepted and the paper he was charged with seized, by which great discoveries were made. He said that our nation was undone, that it was impossible for any succours to be sent to us, as he was informed by the minister that the combined fleet, double the force of ours, had orders to give battle to any British fleet which might attempt getting into the Mediterranean. He said that peace would not be made till Fort St. Phillips was taken, and assured me, tho' he had but twenty battering cannon, he should soon have 180, a great army and the best miners in Europe, and that the place would certainly be warmly attacked, that it would be humane to save the effusion of blood, that General Murray had already acquired enough glory and a great reputation to arms, that there were modes of giving up places honourably.... and that it was a pity to sacrifice so many brave men. I told him that whatever might be the event, it was the duty of a soldier to submit to his fate; that I knew there was not any place impregnable, and that he might ruin our works with a numerous train of artillery; yet I was sure our defence would be such as would always entitle us to an honourable capitulation, but not to flatter himself with the hopes of obtaining the place by any other means, and that a siege was what General Murray ardently wished. The Duke said that if I thought the negotiation would not succeed I need not mention the affair to General Murray. I begged to be excused, and said it was my duty to lay his proposition before General Murray, and to communicate to him every word which had passed betwixt his Grace and me, which I assured him I would accordingly do.... The Duke hinted that there were some private transactions carried on when St. Phillips Castle was taken by the French in '56, and that Admiral Byng had not deserved so cruel a fate.... The above I communicated to General Murray on my return from Mahon.[15]

When the conversation was reported to him, the irascible General Murray, who kept his cool remarkably well for once, in public at least, sent a cold, measured reproof to the Duke:

Monsieur

Lorsqu'il fût proposé à votre brave ancêtre par son souverain d'assassiner le Duc de Guise, il rendit la résponse

10

que vous auriez dû faire quand le Roi d'Espagne vous chargez
d'assassiner le caractère d'un homme dont la naissance est aussi
illustre que la vôtre, ou celle du Duc de Guise.
Je ne puis à l'avenir avoir d'autre communication avec vous
qu'avec les Armes ....

[Sir,
When your gallant ancestor was asked by his King to murder the
Duc de Guise, he made the reply which you should have made
when the King of Spain asked you to murder the character of a
man whose birth is at least as noble as yours, or of the Duc de
Guise.
In future, I cannot have any other communication with you except
in battle.]

The Duke replied with great dignity, accepting the rebuke,
and the siege continued. There is an interesting parallel here with
the Duke's actions later at the siege of Gibraltar, when he sent the
Governor, General Eliott, presents of food. Eliott was quick to
reciprocate with a present of his own of food for the Duke, to
demonstrate that the garrison was well provided, and his reply must
have convinced the Duke that to attempt to bribe him was equally
futile.

It was soon obvious that Don's misgivings, reflected in his
honest reply to de Crillon, were justified. The enemy forces were
soon reinforced by French troops, and the weight of artillery
surrounding the fortress was impressive - 168 guns and several
mortar batteries. Murray sent out a successful sortie, which
destroyed one Spanish battery and took 100 prisoners, and de Crillon
responded by attempting to mount a full blockade.

Within the fortress, things were not going well; scurvy, and
later 'putrid fever,' which was probably typhus, appeared. Most of
the garrison, including the Governor, were affected, and many died,
and soon there were not enough men who were fit enough to man
the defences.

This was George Don's first experience of the horrors of
epidemic disease in an enclosed and beleaguered community; he
was later to face this problem during two campaigns in the Low

11

Countries and when he was in charge of the evacuation of Walcheren in 1809. It was only natural, therefore, with all this behind him, that when he arrived in Gibraltar in the middle of a yellow fever epidemic in 1814, he should have acted so decisively to protect the garrison and the civilian community against the threat of further epidemic disease.

Another factor which added to the difficulties of the defenders was the profound antipathy which arose between Murray and his deputy, Lieutenant General Sir William Draper. Initially, Murray seems to have appreciated Draper's help, but Draper was undermining him behind his back; shortly after de Crillon's attempt to bribe Murray, Sir William wrote to Lord Holderness complaining of Murray's behaviour as a magistrate: '... I hold it incumbent upon me to bring him to trial for the same, and I must beg the favour of you to inform His Majesty therewith.'

Draper had acquired a certain military reputation after leading the successful attack on Manila in 1763, when he was in the service of the East India Company. Later, he engaged in a public controversy with the anonymous author of the *Letters of Junius*, in which he defended the Marquis of Granby, and later himself, against the attacks of Junius, and he had thus also acquired a certain reputation as a journalist as a result.

Curiously, nothing like the original complaint which Draper made in his letter to Lord Holdernesse figured in the charges which he did eventually bring against Murray. Mahon, in his biography of his relative, General Murray,[16] raises the possibility that, having failed with Murray, the Spaniards had successfully suborned Draper, and that this was a first attempt to weaken the defenders' resolve, by raising doubts about the integrity of their commander. Draper followed up his complaint by picking quarrels with Murray about his handling of the defence, and demanded a council of war. Later, Draper apparently tried to convince some of the other officers that negotiations should be opened with de Crillon, which suggests that Mahon's theory may be justified. Murray was patient with Draper at first, but eventually had to relieve him of his post. He must have been very suspicious that Draper was attempting to foment a mutiny

12

with a view to surrendering the fortress, because he attempted to obtain a letter which Draper had circulated:

> George Don, Captain, 51st Regiment, swears: That the Governor went to Colonel Pringle's quarters in the Caroline Lunette and asked to see a paper wrote by Sir William Draper, which the Colonel had had. I did not see the paper, but from conversation I gather it contained Sir William's ideas of the then situation, and that he, Sir William Draper, was of the opinion that propositions ought to be made to the Duc de Crillon, desiring a cessation of hostilities for a period of time, and that in case of no succours arriving, to capitulate. The paper was wrote on or about the 14th inst.

Colonel Pringle was directed to obtain Draper's consent to handing the paper over, but Draper objected and withdrew it. There seems little doubt of Draper's guilt, and it is amazing that it was Murray, and not Draper, who had subsequently to face a court martial.

During all this period, Don was kept busy taking messages between Murray and Draper; as a result, he became a key witness in the court martial of Murray, on charges brought by Draper, which took place in London after the siege was over.

The end of the siege could not be long in coming, and on 4th February 1782 Murray sent his proposals for capitulation to de Crillon, who chivalrously allowed the garrison, which by now consisted of 600 invalids, to march out with their arms, with drums beating and colours flying, in recognition of their bravery, but he insisted that they should become prisoners of war.

De Crillon moved onwards to take charge of the siege of Gibraltar, which had been going on unsuccessfully since 1779. He was less fortunate here, and the Rock, under General Sir George Eliott, held out stubbornly until hostilities ceased early in 1783. Gibraltar had been the only success for Britain in a disastrous war which had seen the loss of the North American colonies as well as Minorca.

Don was one of the first of the defenders to be released, in exchange for a previously captured Spanish officer. He was allowed to travel to England carrying a letter from Murray to Lord

13

Hillsborough. In the letter, Murray recounts the distressing events of the siege and the capitulation, adding:

> My aid de camp, Captain Don, will have the honour to present this letter to your Lordship; he is well acquainted with the most minute circumstance relative to the siege; is an intelligent, distinguished officer, and is furnished with all the papers I have, which he will lay before your Lordship if requisite.[17]

It was a sad end to an episode in a disastrous war for Britain. The only bright spot had been the successful defence of Gibraltar by General Eliott, but apart from this, Britain could take some pride in the heroism of General Murray and the Minorca garrison.

NOTES

1. Manuscript annotation in copy of *Sir George Don*, by Sullivan, Jersey 1884, in Edinburgh Castle.
2. Family tree in Anderson Collection.
3. Grant of Arms, 1810.
4. From the Anderson family tree at Anderson House, Fife. Courtesy of Stephen Aynscough..
5. J. Gilhooley, Edinburgh; personal communication.
6. *Dictionary of National Biography*; Gentleman's Magazine, April 1832; Balleine.
7. Grant of Arms, 1810.
   George Don's Arms are: Vert on a fess Argent between three crescents Or, as many mascles sable
   Crest: Out of a mural crown Or a pomegranate, stalk and leaves proper.
   Motto: Non deerit alter aureus.
   The Arms of Sir Alexander Don of Newton Don were similar, but without
   mascles; see Chapter 4.
8. Balfour, p. 18.
9. Marriage Settlement between George Don and Maria Margaretta Murray in Scottish Records Office (GD2/250).
10. Mahon, p. 394.
11. Murray, pp 50-51.
12. Mahon, Chapter XVIII.
13. Letters: Sir George Eliott to General Murray in Gibraltar Government Archives (GGA).

14. The relationship to which de Crillon refers presumably refers to Don's engagement to Maria Murray. Draper also refers to Don as Murray's nephew (see below, Chapter 2).

15. The above, and most of the description of the siege of Fort St Philip and the court martial of General Murray, is from Mahon, Chapters XVIII and XIX, and Fortescue, Vol. III, pp. 299, 408-411.

16. Mahon, pp. 404-405.

17. *Gentlemen's Magazine*, 1782. Vol. 52, p. 161.

Chapter 2

MARRIAGE AND ARMY CAREER

George Don was now back in England, and no doubt after he had delivered Murray's letter to Lord Hillsborough he was quickly reunited with his Maria. But as they prepared for their wedding, there was still a cloud hanging over the Murrays and Don - the court martial of Lieutenant General Murray, Maria's uncle and guardian and Don's patron.

Murray had remained in Minorca to supervise the repatriation of his troops, and to assure himself that the many invalids were being well looked after. Then he sailed to Italy in order to be with his young wife and his son and heir, who had been born shortly before the siege had ended. All these delays in returning to London were for the best of military and personal reasons, but they were a grave political mistake; he should have hastened to England as soon as possible, for in his absence Sir William Draper and his cronies were busily making trouble for him at the Court of King George III. The government of Lord North had fallen as a result of the military reverses, and had been replaced by the anti-war, reformist administration of the Marquess of Rockingham, which was not likely to be sympathetic to General Murray.

On 24 March 1782, Don wrote from London to Murray:

I arrived here on the 19th inst. at six o'clock in the evening, and immediately delivered your despatches and the private letter to Lord Hillsborough. He read them in my presence and expressed his entire approbation of the contents.... I went to the levee. His Majesty inquired particularly about your health, wished it might soon be perfectly re-established, and seemed desirous to see you in England.... The dispute between you and Sir William is a good deal talked of. In general he is greatly condemned and looked upon as a madman, yet I can perceive he has some friends. Last night a total change of the Ministry was announced. The Rockingham party comes in. The Marquis in place of Lord North.... The [regiment of] Scots Greys have been vacant for some time.... It is said his Majesty intends to give you the

16

[colonelcy of the] regiment as a distinguished mark of his approbation of your conduct... [1]

On April 10th [2] Captain Don wrote again to Murray that Sir William Draper had had an audience with the King in which he did his best to prejudice George III against General Murray, and that Draper was constantly trying to injure Murray's character and reputation as an officer. Don adds, optimistically, that Murray's reputation is too good to be damaged by Draper's calumnies, and that 'all he says tends to his own ruin and destruction, which his friends foresee.'

On May 11th, in a further letter, he informed his chief that General Conway (the new Commander in Chief) had commanded him to tell Murray that the King still had the highest opinion of him, 'and that after inquiry he would most certainly bestow on you the great honour which your conduct justly deserved.'

This seems to indicate that the King was favourably disposed towards Murray, and if Murray had returned to England immediately he would have denied Draper, who was a journalist and a consummate publicist, the time and opportunity to publicise his accusations and so inflame matters that a court martial became inevitable.

But Murray did not arrive in London until June. On 7th August a marriage settlement was signed between General Murray as the guardian of Maria Margaretta, and George Don. In this settlement, Maria Margaretta's father, Patrick Murray, 5th Lord Elibank, settled £5000 on his illegitimate daughter – a large sum in those days.[3] The marriage was celebrated in Orr, un sussex: Murray had a property in Sussex, near Battle, where he built his house, which he named Beauport, after the district where he had been quartered in his beloved Quebec, and the two witnesses to the settlement were from Westminster and Hastings.

Townshend, who had replaced Hillsborough as Secretary at War in the new Rockingham administration, was less sympathetic to Murray, who had written to him and the Commander in Chief, General Conway, demanding a public enquiry in which both his behaviour and Draper's would be examined.

17

But the trial, which started on 12th November 1782, and lasted until January 1783, was of Murray and not of Draper, who had formulated twenty-nine charges against his former superior. These charges ranged from serious accusations of extortion of money from the populace, and exaggerating the weakness of the garrison in order to justify surrender to Crillon, to trivial ones, such as that Murray gave orders that guns were not to be fired without orders from the artillery officer. It took four weeks for the prosecution to present their case to the Court.

Captain Don was called upon to give evidence. He defended Murray vigorously, and was later accused by Draper of lying to save his master. Draper, in his account of the trial, tried to cast doubt on Don's veracity:

> To save his General, his benefactor, and uncle, Captain Don boldly steps forth, avows a false return, which he had not the time to correct in fifteen days time: he gives this false return to the Secretary of State: he is asked if he acquainted him with the mistake: he answers, No. [4]

This apparently refers to the accusation that Murray had exaggerated the weakness of the garrison in order to justify the surrender.

Murray, broken by fatigue and illness, made a moving statement, which, because of the weakness of his voice, had to be read out for him by the judge. In the end, he was found not guilty of all but two minor charges, and the reprimand which he received from the King dwelt mostly on Murray's distinguished service, and condemned Draper for his behaviour, rather than Murray.

On February 19th Murray was promoted to full General. He was never given the command of the Greys which he had longed for, but two years later was appointed to the largely honorary post of Governor of Hull. His campaigning days were over; he retired to his Sussex home of Beauport, where he died in 1794.

One can only speculate why James Murray, whose gallant defence of Minorca against hopeless odds gained him widespread public sympathy - he was popularly known as 'Old Minorca' - was not honoured by the nation as he deserved. Blakeney, who had

18

defended Minorca so feebly in 1756 - he was bedridden and senile at the time - received a peerage. Murray's sterling work in Canada went unrecognised, while Amherst, his predecessor, who had done far less, was created a peer and raised to high office.

There is one possible reason for Murray being passed over in this way. The Murray family had been suspected of Jacobite sympathies in the past - James' brother, Alexander, was certainly a supporter of the Stuart pretenders, and this may have influenced many in Court against him. Perhaps de Crillon's intelligence gathering was reliable, and General Murray *did* have powerful enemies at Court. How otherwise is it possible to explain that the court martial of General Murray was allowed to proceed when, if anyone, it was Draper who should have been in the dock?

Is it stretching things too far to wonder whether George Don's connection with the Murray family may have worked against him too? Certainly he did not receive the knighthood that he so richly deserved until late in life - in 1820. By then the last Stuart had been dead for years, but prejudices die harder than people.

George Don was given a brevet majority in November 1783, and then joined the 59th Regiment, where he became a major in 1784. He was posted to Gibraltar, and in 1786, he went on a trip to Morocco and Spain with two other officers. Mrs Don must have been with him in Gibraltar - in 1787 a passport was issued to Major George Don to travel to France, Spain and Italy 'with his family'.[5] The family referred to must have been Mrs Don and her sisters, as the marriage seems to have been childless.

Don left Gibraltar in 1787, and was there again in 1790-91, according to his own account many years later. He purchased the colonelcy of his regiment in 1789. The 59th Regiment left Gibraltar in May 1792. Don also remarks in the same letter that he had first visited Gibraltar in 1777; this must have been on an official mission or possibly a period of leave from his duties in Minorca.[6]

He was given a staff appointment in England in 1792, and in 1793 he was posted with his regiment to Jersey, where he remained for nine months. In that short time he won the affection of the people of the island, and this was to stand him in good stead

19

when he returned in 1806 as Lieutenant Governor. He dealt firmly with a disciplinary problem in his regiment: soldiers had been moonlighting and 'making bad use of the money they earned', and Colonel Don soon put a stop to this.[7] When the 59th moved out of town to camp, the *Gazette de L'ile de Jersey* praised the good order and discipline of the troops, and added: 'All the officers were well-liked, especially Colonel Don, who is a most humane man... the inhabitants have seen him depart with regret. Nothing can console the island for his departure. It would be happy for humanity if all men had the same temper and sentiments.' [8] The States, the parliament of Jersey, presented him with a vote of thanks inscribed on parchment, acknowledging 'the zeal he had shown in maintaining the discipline of the militia.' [9]

After the French Revolution, the British Government had for a long time tried to remain neutral, but now a new French war had started, this time against Republican France. Louis XVI was executed in January, and in February the French Army invaded the Netherlands, which England was bound by treaty to defend, and an expeditionary force under the Duke of York was sent to Holland to repel the French.

Don worked hard to develop the Jersey militia as a force to defend the island. This preoccupation was to continue when he became Lieutenant Governor in 1806. A French invasion of the Channel Islands was always possible throughout the wars with France - in fact, there had been an attempt in 1781. Indeed, the French did not give up their 900-year old claim to *Les Isles Anglo-Normandes* until after World War II.

Later in 1793, Don was sent to Holland to join the Duke of York's army. He held the post of Deputy Adjutant General to another General James Murray - Sir James Murray Pulteney. Later, in 1794, he served as acting Adjutant General. For his services there he was promoted to full Colonel, and later made an Aide-de-Camp to the King. The army returned to England in 1795, after one of the many unsuccessful or inconclusive campaigns in the area; Don was to experience three more during his career - the Helder expedition in 1799, the German campaign of 1805 and the retreat from Walcheren in 1809.

George Don remained on the Continent as Deputy Adjutant General under Colonel Craig during the winter retreat to Germany in 1794. When Craig was recalled to England in 1795, eventually to lead the successful attack on the Cape of Good Hope,[10] Don remained in Germany, still as deputy to the absent Craig. He did not confine himself to the mundane duties of his post, and soon seems to have become a spymaster, translating and passing on to the Duke of York the reports he received from a network of French, Dutch and German spies. He kept up a correspondence with Craig in England, and the latter, at Don's request, unsuccessfully applied for George Don to be appointed A.D.C. to the King, an honour that he did not receive until several years later. In the winter of 1795 Mrs Don, accompanied by her sisters, the Misses Murray, made a hazardous crossing to Germany to be reunited with her husband.[11]

Later, Don was named military commissioner to the Prussian Army, a post which he retained until 1798 when he was recalled to England, promoted to major general, and given the command of the troops in the Isle of Wight.

When he arrived he set about preparing the defences of the island against a possible French invasion, as he was to do later in Scotland and in Jersey. On one occasion he ordered the alarm to be given, as if the enemy invasion was actually beginning, in order to test the state of readiness of the militia.

Many years later, an old inhabitant of the island remembered General Don. John Green was drinking with his friends in the tap-room of a very small ale-house:

> I was in the tap-room on a day when General Don, the Commander-in-Chief of the army in the Isle of Wight, came with a party of officers to inspect the places where there could be any defence made against the enemy. When they dismounted near the entrance of the tap-room, we who were there began to go out to give place for them; but the General ordered us to keep our seats, saying he would not come in if we left on his account. Mrs Groves [the landlady] made an apology, but the General said that he had met with many worse accommodations than that shed [the 'overflow'

21

of the ale-house] was, and he ordered a lunch for his party, and two gallons of beer for us....

General Don was an old warrior, as he told the volunteers he had been a soldier all through the piece, from a drummer-boy to what he then was; indeed, it was certified to by a man who happened to pass through the forest at a time when some of the volunteers were being inspected by the General. The man, being an old soldier, halted a little to see how they performed in their manual exercise, and seeing the General, he thought he had some knowledge of the person. He asked one who stood by what the General's name was. On being told it was General Don, he asked his Christian name. On being told it was George, 'Then' said he, 'I know him well', and he waited for an opportunity when the word of command was given to 'stand at ease,' to advance and make his 'obedience', and asked him if he remembered such a battle, mentioning the time and place. He (the General) said he would never forget it, for there was such a slaughter that there was but one man left standing beside himself in the company he belonged to. The man answered, 'I know it well, sir. I am that man that stood by you.' The General recognized the man, called him Tom, and shook him by the hand as familiarly as when they were equal in the regiment they had belonged to. He gave him a present, and told the volunteers that they were two that had been through regular soldiering together, and that the man was the drill sergeant when he was in the ranks.[12]

John Green's memory may not have been entirely reliable; there is no evidence that George Don was commissioned from the ranks. The battle referred to must have taken place during the expedition to Holland in 1793.

In 1799 British forces again landed in the Low Countries, this time to attempt to recapture Holland from the French and restore it to the Prince of Orange. Russia had agreed to take part in this campaign, and it was hoped that Prussia would join in against Napoleon.

Don was given the command of a division consisting of two battalions each from the 17th and the 44th regiments, under Sir David Dundas. These troops were raw and inexperienced, having been drawn mainly from the militia, and their equipment was poor. The army landed on the Helder peninsula on 28th August. A lieutenant of the 20th recalled the landing:[13]

> We landed without our baggage on a cold rainy night, and were on the bare sands with little food and no wood. General Don had a nice little cart with his things in, in which he was to sleep, and I recollect envying him when he said, 'Now gentlemen, we halt here; *make yourselves comfortable!*'

There were initial successes, in which Don's men played their part. These included the battle of Oude Karspel, led by Pulteney's column, which was formed by brigades led by Don and Sir Eyre Coote, when the redoubt was carried and 1700 casualties were inflicted on the enemy. Abercrombie's column was also successful, and the engagement was only prevented from being a complete victory by the demoralised retreat of the allied Russian troops, which caused the Duke to hastily order a retreat from Oude Karspel. Don himself recorded much later that 'he was publickly mentioned for his conduct in the action of the 19th September.'[14]

In a further attack, Don's brigades covered the British left to the shores of the Zuyder Zee. A successful attack caused the French to abandon Oude Karspel again. They retired to a shorter line of defence, to await reinforcements.

As the campaign progressed, however, the French gained the upper hand. News of French victories elsewhere on the Continent, and a shortage of supplies, led the Commander in Chief, the Duke of York, and Sir Ralph Abercrombie to seek an armistice. They sent George Don and another officer, Major Spencer Vassal, to the French General Brune, to seek a truce and negotiations towards a British withdrawal. Carola Oman[15] describes what happened:

> General Don, a very absent-minded gentleman... had been sent to the French camp by the Chief, with some despatches, and when pulling them out of his pocket had also pulled out, much to his surprise, yard upon yard of orange ribbon. A large quantity of this had been supplied to the troops of the Secret Expedition, together with proclamations, for distribution among the Dutch. General Don, when searched, was found to have many such inflammatory documents about him.

Don and his companion were arrested as suspicious characters, and his horse was returned by the French to the British lines. Whether or not the discovery and his arrest were due to Don's absent-mindedness - he certainly showed no signs of this in his subsequent career - there is no doubt that Don had been given an undercover mission to the Batavian Directory, to tempt them away from their allegiance to France.[16] Abercrombie had sent him to Brune requesting that he be given a passport to go to the Hague on a mission to the Batavian republican government, and Brune, on discovering the proclamation he carried, arrested him as a spy:

> Yesterday morning [October 8th] General Don was sent to my headquarters in Beverwijk, and I made him aware how vile his action was for a soldier. After seeing what he carried, I had to make him a prisoner of war... Up to now, the Duke of York has not asked for him back. [Brune to Daendels].

> This General Don carried a proclamation to the Batavian Government, requesting that they expel the French and unite their forces with the Prince of Orange... general Don and his deputy [Major Spencer Vassal] are guarded by six grenadiers and an officer until the Duke reclaims them. They will not be returned without advantageous conditions. [Rostollant to General Vandamme]

Don himself remarked later [17] that Brune had told him that he had come over only 'pour paralyser' the French army, and that on one point in the discussion he had laid his hand on his sword when he was tempted to chastise some brutal observation of the Marshal's. It is likely that Brune was aware of Don's intelligence-collecting activities after the previous British campaign in the Netherlands, and that this aroused his suspicions even before he discovered the documents which Don had been carrying.

In the event, Don remained a prisoner. He and Major Vassal were exposed to every indignity, and twice led out for execution. The negotiations for withdrawal were carried out on the British side by Major General Knox, and the British force withdrew. Don was held captive until June 1800, when he, General Hermann (who had been captured in the action of September 19th) and General Mack were exchanged for the French Generals Colly, Grouchy and Perignon.

Don's reputation does not seem to have been harmed by this incident. An acquaintance wrote many years later that he 'became conspicuous in consequence of maintaining some hazardous and delicate communications with the Enemy,'[18] and during his captivity, on November 22 1799, he was granted the colonelcy of the 7th (9th) West India Regiment, succeeding Sir John Moore. On his return to England he rejoined the staff at the Horse Guards, as deputy adjutant -general.

At about this time, he was appointed to command troops (mainly militiamen) in Scotland, organising the defence against a possible invasion by Napoleon. Miller, in *the History of Dunbar*, states that Major General Don was in charge of the greatest military force which had been assembled in the area in recent times. They were encamped on West Barn Links, near Dunbar. The regiments consisted of the Lanarkshire, Perthshire and Fife militias; the Galloway militia as gunners, and a few dragoons to do the general's duty.

Later on, the same author writes that as a result of Don's efforts Dunbar was now well prepared to meet the threatened invasion, and a more vigilant officer than General Don could not have been appointed. He adds that Don had already been severely wounded in active service.[19] This last statement may be correct, but it is not clear in which campaign Don had received a wound.

As he did later in Jersey, Don took a great interest in the organisation of the volunteer regiments, and issued detailed instructions for their assembly in the event of an invasion. He interested himself in the minutiae of procurement of equipment. He also contributed a generous sum - 30 guineas - towards the purchase of this equipment.

Captain Henderson met him in 1802 in Dumbarton, when Don was in the process of reducing Henderson's regiment, the Argylls. The officers dined the major general: 'General Don dined with us the day before this sort of moral execution. He was chatty

25

and good humoured...' He told them the anecdote of his capture by the French quoted earlier, and

> spoke of Canada, of the severity of the frosts there, that for so many months the ground could not be opened. Maclean, whose art in trotting, as it is now called, was impervious to Circumstances, was near trotting the General by a timid sort of Enquiry as to the disposal of the dead during these months? The General was reflecting for a reply, but I being Vice-Chairman diverted it by laughing at Maclean's joke.
>
> The next morning [3rd July 1802] we were reduced after receiving many compliments from General Don.

Henderson made a small ink sketch of Don.[20] Don had never been to Canada, and may have just been retelling one of his uncle General Murray's anecdotes, which would explain why he was at a loss for a reply to the junior officer's facetious query.

Don was promoted to Lieutenant General in 1803, and in 1805 he was made Colonel of the 96th Foot. At about this time he was given the command of a force which included the King's German Legion. This regiment had been formed in 1803, and was mainly recruited from the King's Hanoverian subjects and other German recruits.

The British hoped to take advantage of the fact that Napoleon had had to withdraw most of his troops from the area in order to use them against Austria, and it was planned to send this force to North Germany to recover Hanover, of which George III was Elector, which had been occupied by France, and to prevent its occupation by Prussia, whose ruler had been flirting with Napoleon. If they were successful they would then push on into Holland.

Don had originally been ordered to go on ahead of his troops to Berlin to sound out the Prussian Court on their reaction to the landing of a British force in North Germany, and to obtain the consent of Denmark to a retreat through the province of Holstein in case this should become necessary. His contacts with the Prussians while he was Military Commissioner in Germany after the Helder campaign must have made him an obvious candidate for this mission, and if he had not been replaced by Lord Harrowby it is probable that he would have made a success of it.

26

Baron Ompteda, then an officer in the Legion, wrote: [21]

August 13 [1804] - General Don has taken the command of us. He issued a flattering inauguratory order: 'Excellent officers, and gallant men, the composition of the Legion. I look on this in the light of a bill drawn on us. Dishonour it, and you will be bankrupt!' Later he said verbally, 'Now that I have seen the start of the King's German Legion, I wish Buonaparte would come over tomorrow.'

The officers invited him to their new mess: 'On March 4th [1805] the mess-house, only just finished, was handed over for the use of the first line Battalion. I utilised this as a becoming opportunity to invite General Don...' [22]

In the following month, the regiment was ordered to be ready to embark for the Continent, but it was not until November, after many delays and changes of plan, that the army under George Don, 18000 strong, embarked from Ramsgate, with the objective of recapturing Hanover from the French, who were thought to have their hands full with the war against Austria. Lord Harrowby (who had been Pitt's Foreign Minister for a while in the previous year until he was invalided out when he fell down and suffered a severe head injury, which rendered him incapable of working!)[23] was entrusted with the mission to Berlin. Napoleon had sent General Duroc to Berlin to negotiate with Prussia, and the British Government probably thought that a senior diplomat like Harrowby would carry more weight than an obscure Lieutenant General.

Don was ordered to march with his troops to the Elbe. By the time they embarked, it was too late. General Mack had surrendered on October 16th, and well before they reached the Elbe, Napoleon was in control of Vienna. The British force, including the 6000 from the King's German Legion, did not have an easy crossing; a fierce storm blew up, and the transport ships were scattered. Some had to return to England, and others were only saved from being cast up on occupied shores by a providential change of wind. Don was forced to anchor off Cuxhaven on November 17th, and kept there by adverse winds. Eventually, the bulk of the force was able to land on the Hanoverian shore in early December.

27

Lord Cathcart arrived on the 25th, and took over overall command of the force, which was increased to 25000. He established his headquarters in Bremen, and Don moved with his section of the force, which included the Hanoverians, to Verden.

The French had evacuated all their troops from Hanover to prosecute the war with Austria, except for a strong garrison in the town of Hameln, and Don moved with his force to join the Russian General Tolstoy in investing the town, which they hoped to reduce rapidly, and then advance on Holland. By this time it was far too late. The Austrians had capitulated after the 'Battle of the Three Emperors', and the British force was ordered back to England.[24] On his return to England, Don was informed that he had been appointed Lieutenant Governor of Jersey.

NOTES

1. Mahon, p. 419.
2. *Ibid* p 419.
3. Marriage settlement in Scottish Record Office (GD 2/250).
4. Draper, p16.
5. Diary for 1786 and 1787, Gibraltar Government Archives (GGA).
6. Don to Sir George Murray. 6 August 1829. Governor's Letter Books, GGA.
7. *Gazette de L'île de Jersey*, 20 April 1793.
8. ibid. 25 May 1793.
9. Balleine. p. 631.
10. Article on Sir James Henry Craig in the Dictionary of National Biography.
11. Don Papers. British Library, Add. Ms. 46702-46711, 46883, 46884.
12. 'Recollections of Old John Green'. *Isle of Wight Mercury,* 25th June, 2nd July 1890.
13. Oman, p 212.
14. Governor's Letters 30 July 1817, GGA. (See Appendix I).
15. Oman, p 213.
16. Beijnen, *passim.*
17. Capt. Henderson. *My Recollections.* Manuscript, ca. 1836? In Gibraltar Garrison Library.
18. Memoir of Sir George Don by Col. John Drinkwater Bethune. Manuscript in Gibraltar Garrison Library.

19. Miller, pp174, 177.
20. Henderson, *op cit.*
21. Ompteda. p 176
22. *Ibid.* p 180.
23. *Dictionary of National Biography*, Article on the first Earl of Harrowby.
24. Fortescue, Vol V, pp 285ff; Taezner, M. King's German Legion website. (http://www.kgl.de).

Chapter 3

JERSEY
1806-1809

George Don was appointed Lieutenant Governor and Commander-in-Chief of Jersey on 26 April 1806. The Governor was John Pitt, Earl of Chatham, but he was an absentee Governor, who remained in London throughout, and seems to have taken no interest in the affairs of the island. Don was to be in effective command of Jersey and its forces during his stay there.

Don had already shown a great interest in the defence of Jersey and the militia when he was in Jersey with his regiment, the 59th Foot, in 1792. When he left in April 1793, the States (the Jersey Parliament) had presented him with a vote of thanks inscribed on parchment, which acknowledged 'the zeal he had shown in maintaining the discipline of the militia.'

From this previous postings Don knew how important an effective local militia would be if he was to repel a likely French invasion, and even before he arrived to take up his post he had been in correspondence with officials in Jersey, and was pressing the British Government to provide for the appointment of more instructors for the militia, which would be the main force to defend the island against a French attack, which was expected sooner rather than later. He was successful in his plea, and three further instructors were authorised, so that there would be one for each regiment of militia, and the pay was increased. He found on his arrival that only one of the six regiments of militia was fit for service. He again made a point of increasing discipline, and provided drill sheds for every parish, so that drill could be continued daily whatever the weather.

He also revived the order that all boys between the ages of fourteen and seventeen were to be drilled in preparation for joining the force when they were old enough, and he formed the older boys into a militia regiment of their own. He persuaded the States to produce silver spoons – 'military prize spoons' - for presentation to the men of militia yearly as prizes for marksmanship. With the aid of Lieutenant Colonel La Couteur, the Inspector of Militia, he converted this part-time army into an efficient fighting force.[1]

There was also an urgent need to improve communications in the island, so that the militia could move speedily to repel an attack at any point of the coastline. The roads at the time were no more than muddy tracks, often flooded, through which it would have been impossible to move troops rapidly to the site of a possible invasion. Lyte, in his *Sketch of the Island of Jersey* [1] writes: 'The roads are very bad, and sunk so low that they act as drains to the adjoining fields, and in winter nearly impassable.' Another contemporary author remarks

> The ancient communications in the island in the name of roads are numerous, but narrow, winding, and... very intricate They are sunk below the level of the land, flanked by enormous mounds... which are crowded with trees over-canopying the road... Two carts meeting each other cannot pass; one or other must back to the nearest field or gateway. To this...may perhaps in part be attributed the remarkable proficiency of the Jersey populace in swearing.[2]

The States increased the tax on spirits in August with a view to raising money for road construction, no doubt at Don's behest, and announced that the first road, from St Helier to Grouville, would be named *La Route Don.*

There was strong opposition to this plan in many quarters, especially from the farmers, who would lose land when the roads were widened. The construction of this first road was held up for a time by a farmer who threatened to shoot the first man to touch his land. General Don came himself, in full uniform, picked up a spade, and dug through the bank at the side of the road. The farmer did not fire.

The second road, from St. Ouen's church to Beaumont, was paid for by a grant of £1000 from the British Government, and opened in May 1808. The initial financing of the reform of the road system from liquor taxes was found to be insufficient; and the British Government refused to provide more money, as did the States, so

Don raised a public subscription - he contributed the sum of £100 himself, far more than any other single subscriber, and instituted a lottery - a recourse that he was to return to in Gibraltar - in order to pay for the continuation of the road-building plan.

By this means the third road, from St Helier's to St Aubin, was built; it was opened in November 1809, just after Don had left for Walcheren. Hitherto the only means of communication between the two communities had been on foot across the sands of St. Aubin's Bay.

An objection which was raised at the time was that better roads would in fact help an invading enemy to advance rapidly. One rector, it is said, preached against it from the text 'The broad road leadeth to destruction.'

Davies[3] commenting on this argument, which was resuscitated by WT Inglis in his book The Channel Islands (1834), remarks:

> Once again he missed the point. Don's intentions ... were always to prevent a powerful landing anywhere on the beaches of the Island by having the ability speedily to transport defending forces to wherever they might suddenly be needed.

Work was started on the road-building project a mere five weeks after Don's arrival, and by the time he left Jersey in 1814, eighteen major roads had been built, as well as many connecting roads.

Don's plan for the defence of Jersey therefore depended on rapid communications to allow the defending forces to be mobilised at the first sign of a possible invasion. With this in mind, he established a system of signals and lookout ships which would allow the news of a French fleet leaving St. Malo or any other port to be flashed to Jersey and thence to Guernsey, where a British fleet was stationed, within fifteen minutes. The messages were to be transmitted by flags in the daytime, and by blazing barrels of tar at night.

Don was very conscious of the proximity of the French coast and the danger of an invasion. In this he followed the advice of Colonel John Humfrey, who had been involved in preparing the defences of Jersey since his arrival in 1800. In 1806 Don wrote to the Board of Ordnance [4]

> Colonel Humfrey is of the same opinion with myself respecting the expediency of fortifying the Small Bays and Creeks in this island and when you consider that we are within thirteen miles of the French Coast and exposed to an attack in spite of our Navy. I am sure you will concur with us on this subject.

He was therefore particularly careful to repair the chain of Martello towers and all the other defences which stretched around the shores of the island; but the greatest work of fortification undertaken at the time was the building of Fort Regent, overlooking St. Helier. To be sure, this was not Don's idea - plans had been prepared for the fortress long before Don came on the scene, under the previous Governor, General Conway, and much of the credit for the work must go to Colonel Humfrey, who was the architect of the scheme, a fact which Don was the first to recognise publicly. Within a few days of landing in Jersey, he wrote to Humfrey:

> I do not delay expressing to you the great satisfaction I had this day in examining your plan for fortifying the Town Hill and having maturely considered every part of the ground I am of the opinion that the works could not be more judiciously chosen.

It was, however, Don who laid the foundation stone in 1806. In the ensuing years it was Don who provided the support which Humfrey needed and the energy which saw the fort completed before he left for Gibraltar in 1814. The great mass of Fort Regent looms over and dominates the town of St. Helier. It was designed as a stronghold to be held in the face of any invading force which might succeed in establishing itself on the island. A year after its completion, Napoleon had been finally defeated at Waterloo, and Fort Regent and all the other defences which had been built by Don were never put to the test.

Don was less successful when he attempted to alter the constitution of Jersey. He had always taken a great interest in the deliberations of the States, and frequently sat next to Sir John Dumaresq, the Baillie or President of the Assembly, and listened intently to the proceedings. He spoke fluent French, and would have missed little of what was said.

One Thomas Anley had become Constable of St. Helier, and in December 1807 he was elected to the States with an overwhelming majority. The Court refused to swear him in, because he had been fined twice in the past for 'indecent reflections on the authorities'. Don, obviously afraid of Jacobin influences in the island, asked for a Royal Commission, which recommended that Jurats should in future be selected by the members of the States and by officers of the Crown, but the Privy Council, perhaps wisely, refused to ratify this innovation.

In 1809, Jersey was preparing to celebrate the Golden Jubilee of King George III, and Don *'qui était attaché de coeur et d'âme au trône et à la Patrie'*, was engaged in preparing a programme for the festivities with his usual energy. There were to be salvos and feus de joie from vessels commanded by his Serene Highness Admiral the Duke de Bouillon, a procession to St. Helier Church, a sermon, a dinner and ball by subscription, and fireworks, while all the inhabitants of St. Helier were to be required to illuminate their homes. An address was to be sent to the King.

While these celebrations were being prepared, Don received a despatch from Lord Castlereagh ordering him to take command of the troops in Walcheren, an island in the mouth of the River Scheldt in the Netherlands. The States met as soon as the orders for Don arrived. They sent an address to the King, which praised Don in the highest terms, and regretted his departure They begged the King to allow him to return as soon as possible. They also voted 200 guineas for a piece of silver, which they presented to their Lieutenant Governor in recognition of his great services to the island.

Lieutenant General Don left Jersey on the 16th October 1809 on the frigate *Daphne*, and Major General Leighton took temporary command of the island. In the speech which he made on assuming command, he remarked that in view of the work already done by Don, little remained to be done for the well-being and defence of the island, and that his aim would be to continue with

34

Don's measures, which had the general approval of the inhabitants of the island.

One week later, the celebrations for the Golden Jubilee began, but Don was on the high seas, on his way to Walcheren, to save what he could from the disaster that he was to find there.

Sullivan remarks at the end of his account of Don in Jersey[1] that his favourite phrase to his opponents was '*Je vous ferai du bien malgré vous*' – 'I will do you good whether you like it or not,' and that he was insulted and on the point of being drummed out of the island by a ferocious lynch mob because of some of the innovations which he had introduced. Whether he was exaggerating or not, there is no doubt that Don's innovations, and especially his road-building, activities, aroused a great deal of opposition on the island. But he relied on the support of such influential local men as the Baillie, Sir John Dumaresq, and officers like Colonels La Couteur and Humfrey, and in the end his success spoke for itself, when the Jersiais realised that he *was* 'doing them good,' and the opposition evaporated and was replaced by a warm regard, as the inhabitants came to understand his true motives. Then they realised with what energy he had protected them against invasion, and that in the process he had provided them with a modern road system and many other benefits.

NOTES

1. Sullivan, *passim.*
2. Quayle, *Agriculture in the Islands,* quoted in Syuret and Stevens, p. 219.
3. Davies.
4. PRO WO55/808
5. Balleine.

Chapter 4

WALCHEREN AND JERSEY
(1809-1814)

The British Cabinet, anxious to be seen to carry the war to Napoleon, had been considering a landing on the island of Walcheren, at the mouth of the River Scheldt in the Low Countries, since early in 1809. The primary aim of the expedition was to destroy the French squadron at Flushing, the shipbuilding yards there and at Antwerp, and to block the Scheldt to ships of war. Initially, troops were not available for this enterprise, but by the middle of May an army had been assembled. The Earl of Chatham was offered the command of the troops, while Rear Admiral Sir Richard Strachan was to command the fleet.

The greatest force ever to have left England – 40000 men - was embarked on July 27th, and the landing was made successfully. At first the expedition went well; the town of Middleburgh surrendered on July 31st, and the port of Flushing was captured after a short siege. Soon the whole island of Walcheren was in the hands of the British forces, and plans were being made to advance towards Antwerp.[1]

But all was not well. An epidemic of 'miasmatic fever' (generally thought to have been typhus, but a recent author [2] has suggested that the epidemic might have been a combination of typhus, typhoid, malaria and dysentery) spread rapidly among the troops; by August 28th there were 4000 men sick. Chatham, who was not getting on well with Strachan, dithered, and then returned to England on September 14th, leaving the island under the command of Sir Eyre Coote.[3] The number of cases continued to rise; there were 11000 by September 7th, and 1000 men had died in the first four weeks.

It was clear that Walcheren would have to be abandoned, and George Don was sent for by the Commander-in-Chief, Sir

36

David Dundas, to organise the evacuation of the troops. He arrived on the frigate *Daphne* from England on October 24th. He immediately took personal charge of the arrangements for the care of the sick soldiers, and inspected the hospitals in which they were being treated. By the 26th, first the ill men and then the convalescents were being embarked, and Don reported to Lord Liverpool that the garrison was in such a depleted state that he could barely protect even Flushing from an attack by the French. He added that there was no chance of any of the soldiers recovering enough ever to take the field again unless they were removed from Walcheren immediately. He judged that even of the so-called fit men, only one third were capable of fulfilling their duties.

On the 30th, Don held a meeting with Rear Admiral Otway, the Earl of Dalhousie,[4] and the exhausted Sir Eyre Coote, who wrote: 'Something must be done, or the British nation will lose the British Army – far more valuable than the island of Walcheren.' He handed over command on November 2nd to perhaps the only man who could do something – Don - and sailed for England with Dalhousie.

Officially, it was not yet admitted that the forces were being withdrawn from Walcheren, but it was easy to guess that this would happen. Captain Paget of the *Revenge* wrote home on November 16th. [5]

> To this moment General Don is carrying on the Humbug of keeping & defending this Island against any force which can be brought against it, & the curious thing is that there are so many Gulpins who swallow it all. Whereas, I know that the arrangements are making for the embarkation of the wretched remnant of the army, as also the means preparing for the destruction of the magnificent Wet Docks.

He was quite correct.

On December 4th, Mrs. Don, who had come with her husband, embarked with her maid and Don's coach, which he had also brought with him, on *HMS Caesar*,[6] which remained at anchor while Don supervised the evacuation of troops, the

37

dismantling of the defences, and the demolition of the dockyard and storehouses of the port of Flushing.

When the French sent an officer under a flag of truce with a message that they would harass the rear to hinder the embarkation of troops unless Don stopped destroying the dockyard, he answered curtly that if they attempted to carry out their threat, he would open the sluices on them and drown them. Don also suspected that the civil authorities were in collusion with the French, and conspiring with them to attack the remaining British forces as they withdrew from the island, and he made the same threat to them.

> Gen. Don immediately assembled at his quarters the burgomaster and chief burghers; he informed them that in the morrow the evacuation of their island would be effected, and that he would fain hope that no molestation of the French would oblige him to cut the dykes. '*Messieurs*,' said Sir George, with that soldier-like demeanour for which he was remarkable; '*Messieurs – Votre isle existe aujourdhui; mais, si je le trouve apropos, il n'existera plus demain.*' With this significant hint, the conclave was dismissed. Several messengers were afterwards observed to pass and repass between the town and the French head-quarters. On the 23rd December 1809, the British army sailed out of the Scheldt without having lost a man during the embarkation, or any of the vessels receiving a shot from a French battery. [7]

The rest of the army was thus embarked safely, and Don and his retinue boarded the *Caesar*, on the December 9th, while the rearguard, under Lieutenant Colonel Pilkington of the Royal Engineers (who was later to be Don's Chief Engineer in Gibraltar), undermined the gates of the new harbour and blew it up, and burnt all the storehouses to the ground. Don reported to Lord Liverpool:[8]

> The very judicious and skilful manner in which these measures have been completed, reflect great credit on Lieut.-Colonel Pilkington, and the several others who acted with him, and I am persuaded it will afford your Lordship peculiar satisfaction to know, that the whole of this extensive work has been accomplished, without any injury being done to the inhabitants;

the destruction not having been extended beyond what was necessary to deprive the enemy of the advantage of Flushing as a naval station.

... I cannot conclude this report without acquainting your Lordship that I found the army in an excellent state of discipline, and that the conduct of the troops has in every respect merited my warmest approbation. On the day of embarkation, the different corps of the army marched from the several points, and embarked in the most perfect order and regularity; and the magistrates of the towns and villages, expressed to the officers left in charge of the rear guards, that the troops on their departure had in no instance molested or injured the inhabitants.

Don had done what was required of him, and he had done it efficiently and humanely.

In what manner Sir George Don discharged the arduous duty of commanding a large force under such painful and inglorious circumstances, what personal attention he gave to the hospitals and other arrangements for the care and comfort of the suffering troops, it is not necessary here to notice. The surviving officers and soldiers who served in that ill-fated expedition, can never forget the extraordinary exertions and selfless devotion of the gallant chief.[9]

He did not return to Jersey for nearly a year. He must have been in London for the enquiry into the disaster at Walcheren, where Chatham tried to throw the blame on Strachan, who defended himself vigorously. In the end Chatham was cleared of blame by the enquiry, but the Londoners were in no doubt as to where the blame lay:

Lord Chatham with his sword undrawn
Stood waiting for Sir Richard Strachan.
Sir Richard, longing to be at 'em
Stood waiting for the Earl of Chatham,

they sang; or again:

The great Earl of Chatham, with a hundred thousand men,
Sailed off to Holland, and then sailed back again.

While in Walcheren, Don had taken Captain George Arthur into his personal staff. Arthur had been ADC to Don's predecessor, Sir Eyre Coote, and he now returned to Jersey with

39

Don as his ADC and military secretary. As Lieutenant General
Sir George Arthur, his career was to parallel Don's closely. After
a short and relatively undistinguished military career, he was to
find success as a colonial administrator, in British Honduras,
Tasmania, Canada and India, over a period spanning more than
thirty years.

There can no doubt that he learned much from his
association with Don, and indeed the two men maintained a
correspondence until the death of the latter. George Arthur's
Governorships, just like Don's, were marked by the building of
schools, churches, hospitals and roads – in 1825, George Don
was advising him to build roads in Tasmania to open up
communications, as 'you saw in Jersey.' Sir George Arthur's
biographer comments:

Though a loyal and obedient servant of the Crown, he
undoubtedly carried his own ideas to the colonies he ruled over, and
his long career indicates that the policies shaped by those ideas
satisfied his superiors in London.

This comment could equally apply to George Don.[10]

At this time, Don also applied for and received Grants
of Arms for himself and his brothers William and John, and
recorded his arms in the Public Register of All Arms and
Bearings in Scotland.

The arms were: Vert on a fess Argent between three crescents
Or, as many mascles Sable.

Crest: Out of a mural crown Or a pomegranate, stalk and leaves
Proper.

Motto: NON DEERIT ALTER AUREUS (Another golden
branch will succeed).

The Arms of the Dons of Newtondon in Berwickshire,
recorded over a century earlier, are almost the same, but without
mascles. This would suggest that George and his brothers were
related, or at least thought that they were related, to Sir Alexander
Don of Newtondon.[11] Mascles, in heraldry, are hollow diamonds
which symbolize chain-mail, and were thus no doubt chosen
by Don as a symbol of his military career. In Scottish heraldic

40

custom, each bearer of arms adds a distinctive element to his personal arms. A print showing Don reviewing troops in the Isle of Wight, dated 1799 (in the Anderson collection), shows a similar coat of arms, suggesting that there was already a family coat of arms, from which George and his brothers later adapted their own.

Don returned to Jersey and resumed his post of Lieutenant Governor in May 1810, and the militia presented him with the gold-hilted sword which they had promised him before he left for Walcheren (this sword is now in the Scottish United Services Museum in Edinburgh) in recognition of his services to them.

The programme of road-building was continued energetically, and another fifteen main roads were completed in four years. There was a severe storm in 1812, and the sea-wall was breached, threatening large areas of the island with flooding, and Don immediately had the whole sea-wall from St. Helier to Gorey rebuilt.

The work on Fort Regent was also progressing. John le Couteur, then an ensign in the 95th Regiment, of which Don was the Colonel) recorded:[12]

> In 1810 I mounted perhaps the first guard at Fort Regent, for on that day Sir George Don, the Commander-in-Chief (then General Don) came to visit the still unfinished works…

Don asked him what facilities there were for the guard, and on hearing that the guard room furniture was very basic, asked the ensign what furniture he wanted, then tolerantly signed an order for it immediately, which 'made the guard room very snug.'

Shortly after arriving in Jersey, on November 17th 1806, Don had laid the foundation stone at Fort Regent. By the time he left in 1814, the Fort had been largely completed, although some work on it continued for a few years. It was the essential link in the defence of Jersey against the threat of invasion by Napoleon. By 1815, Napoleon was gone, but the Fort still stands, a monument to Don's predecessor, Marshal

41

Conway, to the Engineer, Colonel Humfrey, who conceived the idea and brought it to reality, and to Don himself.[13]

George Don took an intense personal interest in everything which might affect the safety and well-being of Jersey in case of attack or blockade. Concerned about the food supply in time of war, he brought areas of waste land into cultivation, in spite of assurances from the locals that the land was useless for growing crops:[14]

In order to evince by actual experiment the practicability of bringing into culture the most arid and hopeless of these wastes, General Don was induced to take into his own hands a small portion of the Quennevais, near its centre, pointed out to him as *le sol plus ingrat...* The vegetable earth, which had been overwhelmed by sand, was discovered from six to ten feet under the surface. This was removed to the surface, and the whole area laid level. In Jan. 1812 ten vergées were sown with rye without any manure. In the Spring buckwheat, peas, tares and lucerne were sown, and potatoes planted. In June white clover and sainfoin. The motive for diversifying these experiments was to bring conviction to the incredulous that this bleak and dreary region is really capable of producing a variety of plants. To this smiling spot the General gives the appropriate term of the Oasis. All the product is of superior quality.

The area, which is now a housing estate, has been known as Don's Farm ever since.

Quayle adds

Every day gives proof of the interest taken in the welfare of Jersey, by its resident Governor; it is probable that during the seven years since his appointment, more has been actually done for its security and improvement, than by any other individual during more than as many centuries, elapsed since it being under British rule...

He lists the improvement to the militia, the defences and the roads, and continues:

...As a farmer, the General has also led the way, shewing by demonstration, *at his own expense* [my italics], and by his own example, how an important benefit may be conferred on the

42

island, by reclaiming the most neglected part of it. These are the acts of one energetic mind, prompted by a sense of duty...

He adds that Don's opponents were converted to advocates when they realised his sincerity and 'his perfect disinterestedness.'

However, Don did not always have the unquestioning support of the Jersiaise. Radicals had been elected to the magistracy, and were re-elected when he refused to confirm their appointments, and resolutions were passed attacking the control of the island by the Westminster. Fearing that 'in a few years the bench will be filled with very improper people,' he asked for a Commission of Enquiry into the electoral arrangements, but got little response out of the British Government.

One of Don's main concerns at this time, as seen in his letters, was to obtain reliable intelligence of the intentions of the French. He had to rely on spies who infiltrated across the water into France, but who seem to have been largely ineffectual. He was always concerned for the safety of these men he sent to France, many of whom were caught by Napoleon's secret police. In one of his letters to Sir John Doyle, Lieutenant Governor of Guernsey, he writes (24th July 1813):[15]

> I heartily hope that this will be the last enterprize of the kind, that we may have to execute. The people employed in it are exposed to great danger, and no good can possibly arise in the present state of things from employing such emissaries.

He was probably hindered more than he was helped by the indefatigable Philippe Dauvergne, a Jerseyman who had been adopted by the Duc de Bouillon (who had the same surname) before the latter's death in 1792, and who styled himself Prince de Bouillon as a result. This colourful character, with his own team of spies, was continually hatching plots against Napoleon, including one to kidnap him, but the Emperor and his agents were always ahead of him, and he got nowhere. After Napoleon's defeat at Waterloo, Dauvergne hoped to be proclaimed ruler of Bouillon, which had been a semi-independent Duchy throughout the Middle Ages; but the Congress of Vienna thought otherwise, and gave the territory to the Netherlands. The disappointed Dauvergne died soon afterwards, it is said by his own hand.[16]

In 1813, because of a lack of small change in the island, the States voted to issue silver tokens as currency, and when Don approved the measure, and obtained permission from London, these tokens were coined, and remained in circulation until 1834, when British currency became the official coinage of Jersey. A few years later, Don was to propose an issue of tokens in Gibraltar, presumably for the same reason, but on this occasion London did not give approval, and an unofficial token was issued by a local businessman, as had happened on several occasions in previous years.

A census of Jersey had been made in 1806, shortly after Don's appointment as Lieutenant Governor. In 1814 he ordered another census (it was actually carried out in 1815, after he had left Jersey). This second census was carried out specifically to determine the manpower available for the militia in the event of a French invasion.[17]

Don later recorded that he had been of assistance to the Duc de Berry in 1813 while the latter was in Jersey, and the Duke presented him with a magnificent sporting gun, now in the Scottish United Services Museum in Edinburgh, in 1814, possibly in thanks for his help in getting the Duke across to Normandy after Napoleon's first abdication and exile to Elba.[18]

In 1814 George Don was appointed Lieutenant Governor of Gibraltar, replacing Lieutenant General Colin Campbell, who had died after a long illness, following an attack of yellow fever during the epidemic of the previous year which he had survived, but which had left him severely debilitated. At the same time Don was promoted to General.

Although some of Don's actions in Jersey were unpopular with some sections of the population, there is no doubt that most of the Jersiaises appreciated him as a man

44

devoted to their welfare. The States addressed him in glowing terms on his departure.[19]

Surrounded as they are by lasting memorials of his love for their land, the States recognise that no one ever won a better right to their esteem. He is one of that small group of distinguished men, whose work has made an epoch in the history of Jersey. In the short space of eight years he has changed the face of the country. He has made our coast-line bristle with forts, ramparts and batteries, in which more than 600 cannon secure us from invasion. He has brought the Militia to its present state of perfection. In spite of obstacles which would have daunted a less determined man, new roads have been cut and old ones remodelled from one end of the island to the other. Works wisely conceived and rapidly erected have saved the richest part of our soil from inundation by the sea. His mind has been constantly occupied with plans to increase our prosperity, and to accomplish this he has not scorned to attend to the smallest details. Nothing could quench his ardour or turn him from his task. To these rare qualities his Excellency has added a marked consideration for this assembly and a most touching affability towards all classes of the population.

They asked him to have his portrait painted at their expense while he was in London. Don's reply, acknowledging their request, summarises the benefits which he had brought to Jersey:

When placed in command of the Island of Jersey, it became my fixed resolution to devote myself to two objects: the actual security of the Island, and the permanent welfare of its inhabitants. The strength and happiness of a country are essentially connected with its agricultural industry, to which the most powerful stimulus is a certain and ready market. By the communications opened throughout the island for military purposes, the husbandman has enjoyed the advantage of easy conveyance to the towns and harbours, and the same communications will also afford facilities for bringing the waste lands into culture at a cheap rate.

The solid works constructed in the sea, while they serve as a bulwark against the invading enemy, protect fertile lands from

45

inundation; and the other measures adopted have aimed, in the same measure at twofold benefits in war and peace....

He is full of good advice for the future; he begs them to keep the fortifications in good repair, and to keep up the training of the youth for the militia.

The strong fortress lately constructed in the island, will ensure to its inhabitants the greatest blessing - the protection of Great Britain for ever... the improvement of the Civil jurisdiction and policy has been the object of my constant solicitude.

No doubt reflecting on the problems he had had with 'improper persons' being elected to public office, he threw out recommendations for changes to the method of electing Jurats and representatives. He also informed the States that the Prince Regent had agreed that the new fortress overlooking St. Helier should be named Fort Regent.

Later, he wrote again that he had approached Thomas Lawrence (later Sir Thomas Lawrence, PRA) to paint his portrait, but had found that the sittings would take up too much of his time. Typically of the man, he recommended that the States should instead spend the money that they had put aside for the portrait on improving the new roads.

The portrait that hangs in Queen Elizabeth Castle (by George Watson) was acquired much later, but was probably painted earlier. It shows Don in an uncharacteristically martial pose, and was acquired for Jersey in 1938.[20]

Several places in Jersey are named after Don: Don Street (near the site of his residence, where Woolworth's now stands), Don Road and Don Farm, among others. The chief monument to Don in Jersey, however, is the statue standing in St Helier's Royal Parade Gardens. It was originally proposed in 1832, after his death, but it was not until 1872 that the States commissioned a French sculptor, Robineau, to cast the statue. It was finally completes and unveiled in 1885.

The Parade Gardens are named after the parade ground which George Don had created when he ordered a sandy waste to be levelled – an interesting precursor of his action in Gibraltar

46

in developing the area around the Grand Parade into the Alameda Gardens.

NOTES

1. Fortescue. Vol vii, p 90 ff.
2. Howard, M. Walcheren 1809: a medical catastrophe. *British Medical Journal* Vol 319 pp 1642-5 (1999).
3. General Sir Eyre Coote was the nephew of the famous general of the same name who distinguished himself in the Indian campaigns. He had fought by the side of Don in the Helder expedition ten years previously. In spite of his increasing eccentricity, he was appointed deputy to Lord Chatham at Walcheren.
4. The ninth Earl of Dalhousie was the father of the better-known tenth Earl, who became Governor-General of India.
5. Lord Hylton.
6. Richardson, W. p. 278.
7. United Services Journal, 1832, pp.227-228..
8. Letter: Don to Lord Liverpool. Reproduced in the *London Gazette*, December 30th 1809.
9. United Services Journal, 1832, p. 227
10. Shaw. Pp. ix-x.
11. Burnett, C.J. Scottish United Services Museum, Edinburgh: Personal communication, May 16th 1995.
12. Stevens, p 14.
13. Davies, passim.
14. Quayle,. pp 71, 229. Don retained his interest in agriculture in Jersey even after he left: He ordered 4 copies of this work, via the Gibraltar Garrison Library, in 1816, shortly after it was published.
15. Société Jersiaise. Miscellaneous Papers.
16. Syuret, M, and Stevens, J. p. 221.
17. Société Jersiaise website. Glendenning, A. *General Don's Militia Survey of 1815.*
18. Wood, S. Scottish United Services Museum, Edinburgh: Personal communication November 20th 1997. See also Appendix I
19. Société Jersiaise. Pamphlets.
20. Société Jersiaise. Miscellaneous Papers.

Chapter 5

GIBRALTAR – AND SAN ROQUE

George Don arrived in Gibraltar Bay on HMS *Edinburgh* on 9th October 1814. Once again he was Lieutenant Governor to an absentee Governor. This time it was Edward, Duke of Kent, the fourth son of George III, who had been removed from Gibraltar in 1802 following a mutiny in the garrison provoked in part by his excessive harshness, but who retained the title of Governor until his death in 1820, not long after he had fathered an heir to the throne, the future Queen Victoria.

Gibraltar was to be Don's home for the rest of his life. For most of the time, he held supreme power as Lieutenant Governor over the town and Garrison. The Duke of Kent retained the title of Governor – and the salary – but he was never allowed to take any part in the governance of Gibraltar, nor indeed to have any other official post, until the day he died.

At the time that Don arrived in Gibraltar to take up the post of Lieutenant Governor, he was still plain General Don. He had been awarded the Royal Guelphic Order, a Hanoverian order of knighthood that, as it was not a British decoration, did not entitle him to be addressed as Sir George Don, and he felt strongly that he had been passed over, and that he had been cheated of the GCB that he had been promised for his sterling work in extricating the British expeditionary force from the disaster that the Walcheren expedition had become in the hands of the Earl of Chatham.[1]

One may speculate why Don was passed over for so long. His relatively humble origins may have worked against him, or the Government may have been anxious to play down Don's role at Walcheren, in order to avoid further embarrassment to itself and to the Earl of Chatham.

As I have suggested earlier, it is not beyond the bounds of possibility that Don's early association with old General Murray and his marriage to his niece, Maria Murray, could have worked against

48

him. Alexander Murray, the General's brother and another of Maria's uncles, had been a well-known Jacobite sympathiser, and even Maria's father, Patrick, 5th Lord Elibank, did not himself escape suspicion of pro-Stuart leanings. Indeed, the last serious attempt – in 1752 - to put Bonnie Prince Charlie on the throne of England was known as 'the Elibank Plot.' When this plot was discovered, Alexander Murray thought it wise to flee to France, where he remained in exile for many years, and Patrick Murray, who must have known of the plot, even if he was not actively involved, was thereafter regarded with grave suspicion.

It was generally thought that General Murray had been deprived of a well-deserved peerage because of this, in spite of his loyalty to the Crown, his sterling work as Governor General of Canada, and his tenacious if unavailing defence of Minorca. Don was loyal to Murray, and this loyalty may well have been held against him. Indeed, he is described as a relative of Murray in the *History of the King's Own Yorkshire Light Infantry*.[2] During Murray's trial, in which Captain Don, as Murray's aide de camp, gave evidence in favour of his superior, Sir William Draper, Murray's arch-enemy, referred to Don as Murray's nephew. [3] These references may only be allusions to his engagement and marriage to Maria Margaretta, Murray's niece, but they serve to indicate how closely Don and Murray were associated in the eyes of those around them. Even years after the last Stuart pretender had died, it is possible that the ancient Jacobite taint in the Murray name may have remained attached to George Don and his wife.

In 1817, the Duc de Berry, with whom Don had worked closely while he was in Jersey, wrote to Don[4] informing him that Louis XVIII had conferred on him the Grand Cross of the Royal Order of Military Merit, which he explained was of equal status to that of St. Louis, which could only be awarded to Catholics.

In May, Don sent his thanks to the Prince Regent, via Lord Bathurst, for permitting him to accept the French honour, and requested permission to add the insignia and that of the Royal Guelphic Order to his armorial bearings.[5] Bathurst apparently gave his blessing, but two months later,[6] Don wrote again complaining that he had received a letter from his friend Goulbourn informing him that Castlereagh had ordered that the permission Don had been given to accept the French decoration was to be withdrawn. This was very embarrassing, Don said, as he had been using the title publicly since April. He enclosed an account of his military service during the Revolutionary War, emphasising his services to the French Royal Family (Appendix I). Bathurst seems to have managed to smooth things over, and Don was allowed to keep the French decoration, after which he always added 'OMM' to his list of decorations, in addition to the GCH. of the Royal Guelphic Order.

In 1820, George Don finally achieved his well-deserved knighthood when he was awarded the GCB. A disappointment was to follow, however. He must surely have realised that he could never expect to supplant a Royal Duke as Governor, but when the absentee Governor, Edward, Duke of Kent, died in 1820, Don might have hoped to be promoted to Governor, but again he was passed over, this time in favour of John Pitt, the 2nd Earl of Chatham, the same man who had been his absentee superior in Jersey, and whose gross incompetence had contributed to the military disaster at Walcheren, when Don had had to be called in to pick up the pieces. But Chatham was a Peer of the Realm, and the son of one great Prime Minister and the brother of another; and George Don's undoubted qualities could not hope to compete with this.

Chatham arrived in Gibraltar in 1821. He left most of the running of the place to his subordinates, the Civil and Military Secretaries, and the constant flow of Governor's letters which had emanated from Don dwindled to a mere trickle. He remained in Gibraltar until 1825, when he left for England, complaining that the weather in Gibraltar did not suit him.

When he last came back, he said it was totally impossible for him to return to Gibraltar, the heat of the climate had disagreed with him to such an extent.[7]

Throughout the Chatham years, Sir George Don remained in the area, but retired completely from public life, spending most of his time in the house he kept in San Roque, or in the Governor's Cottage, near Europa Point, which was the summer residence of the Governors of Gibraltar, and which he had had repaired and extended. He was not completely out of touch, though: one of Lord Chatham's few letters to him, asking him to clear up a question of some property, suggests that he might deal with it 'perhaps when you next come into Town' [8] He probably kept well away from Chatham for most of the time. Don retained only the presidency of the Garrison Library and continued to chair the committee meetings. Lord Chatham was styled the Patron of that institution during his stay in Gibraltar, but he does not seem to have taken any active interest in the Library.

Chatham never returned to Gibraltar after 1825, but like the Duke of Kent previously he still remained Governor, drawing his full pay of £2800 per annum. He seems to have shown little interest in the place, although he did send a donation of £50 for the Poor Fund during the yellow fever epidemic of 1828. Don gladly stepped forward to take up the reins again after Chatham left. He appealed to Whitehall, asking that at least he should be considered for promotion if Chatham were to die (Chatham was a year or two younger than Don).[9] No assurances were forthcoming from Whitehall, and in the event Chatham outlived Don, and remained absentee Governor until his death in 1835 at the age of 79. The then Lieutenant Governor, Sir Alexander Woodford, was promoted to Governor, and the post of Lieutenant Governor fell into disuse.

San Roque

In April 1816 Don reported to Bathurst that he had been unwell, and that his doctor had recommended a sojourn in San Roque: 'The village is situated on Rising Ground and the air of it is considered remarkably pure and healthy.'[10]

The Gibraltarians agreed: for many years before and after, they used to go to San Roque to recuperate after an illness.

George Don's convalescence in the little hilltop town, whence the Spanish inhabitants of Gibraltar had fled in 1704, was probably the initial episode of a love affair between Don and the Campo de Gibraltar area. He lost no time in renting a house in San Roque, which he fitted up with the help of the Barrack Master's

Artificers,[11] and he must have purchased a property there shortly afterwards, as in 1822 he was granted land by the Town Council in order to build an extension to his house.[12] He appears to have spent much of his time in San Roque,[13] and in 1828 the San Roque Town Council took the trouble to record that ``the English Governor of Gibraltar owns his own house in this city, and spends a large part of the year here''.[14]

Earlier, the Council had stated that the house was situated in Calle San Felipe.[15] Don's house in San Roque was acquired after his death by Mr. Francia, a well-known Gibraltar businessman. There is a ruined house known as Villa Francia near to the seaside village of Puente Mayorga, within the municipal limits of San Roque, but this could not possibly have belonged to Don, in view of his praise of the pure air and high ground of San Roque itself, as this area is low-lying, and was widely regarded as unhealthy.[16] Indeed, Lieutenant Colonel Gilbard, in his *Popular History of Gibraltar*, correctly places Villa Francia in the outskirts of Campamento, and General Don's residence within the town of San Roque.[17]

In subsequent chapters we will see how much Don achieved as Lieutenant Governor. Hardly a day went by when he was not sending off several letters to Whitehall, to the British Consuls in Spain and Morocco, to his various civil and military officials in Gibraltar or to private individuals. If he was able to spend a large proportion of his time in San Roque and still get through the volume of work that he did, he must have had an excellent and very overworked courier service with Gibraltar, and his officials must have had to commute regularly between the two towns. He certainly had the road to San Roque improved, and this must have been not only for the use of his coach, but to accommodate the increased traffic that he generated. Indeed, according to Beauclerk,[18] he also instituted a regular stagecoach service between the two towns.

Don's official residence, except while Chatham was in Gibraltar, was of course the Convent, which had been the Governor's official residence since the early days of the British presence in Gibraltar. He also made use of the Governor's Cottage, near Europa Point, which had been built in the early years of the century as the

Governor's summer residence by General O'Hara, to accommodate his second family. Don seems to have used the Cottage as his base in Gibraltar during the Chatham years, and altered and extended it to his taste.

NOTES

1. Don to Bathurst; Don to Sir Henry Bunbury. April 17th 1815. Governors Letters. GGA. See Appendix I.
2. Wylly. Vol I, p118.
3. Draper, Sir W , p 16.
4. Duc de Berry to Don. Governors Letters, February 1st 1817. GGA.
5. Don to Bathurst. Governors Letters, May 2nd 1817. GGA. See Appendix I.
6. Ibid. 30 July 1817.
7. Hay, R.W., giving evidence in the *Report on the Military Expenditure*, House of Commons, 1834, p 1.
8. Chatham to Don. Governors Letters June 1st 1824, November 24th 1824. GGA.
9. Don to Huskisson. Governors Letters. October 28th 1827. GGA.
10. Don to Bathurst. Governors Letters, April 2nd 1816. GGA.
11. Bassett, M. p 13; Munro, C.C. p 11.
12. Caldelas Lopez, p 112.
13. Scott, C.R, pp. 43-44.
14. Caldelas Lopez. p 122.
15. Ibid. p 112.
16. Hennen, p. 12.
17. Gilbard, pp 86, 89.
18. Beauclerk, p. 322.

Chapter 6

THE PUBLIC HEALTH

On his arrival in the Bay of Gibraltar, Don found that an epidemic of yellow fever was raging in the town. He was persuaded by Admiral Fleming not to go into the town until the epidemic had subsided, and he spent his first weeks in Gibraltar on the *San Juan Nepomuceno*, a Spanish hulk which had been captured at Trafalgar and was now used as a store ship.

His stay in the harbour was prolonged by an attack of gout, but he did not allow the time to go to waste. He asked for and received daily reports about the situation in the town, and he began to make plans for the future of his new charge.[1]

The town of Gibraltar, he found, was in a ruinous state. Most of the buildings had been destroyed during the Great Siege, and although this had ended over thirty years earlier, there had been little rebuilding. Gibraltar had enjoyed an economic boom because of the prolonged war against Napoleon. As a result, there was an influx of population from other Mediterranean countries, some of whom were refugees from the French, and others who saw economic opportunities in the flourishing entrepôt trade. Little of the money which came in had been devoted to improvements. One or two impressive town houses had been built by the most successful businessmen, but high rents[2] meant that the bulk of the increasing population was forced to live in indescribable squalor in overcrowded tenements or ramshackle huts.

Gibraltar had been struck by a series of epidemics of yellow fever[3], almost certainly brought over from the West Indies with the increasing sea traffic across the Atlantic. In the first of these epidemics, in 1804, nearly six thousand civilians and soldiers were estimated to have died. This figure may have been exaggerated, and the subsequent outbreaks of 1813 and 1814 had a lower mortality, but Don, who arrived in the middle of the latter epidemic, must have been keenly aware that the defence of Gibraltar would be put at risk if the garrison were to be further weakened by a return of the

54

disease. There was also the commercial aspect: in a circular to the civilian Inspectors of Districts, most of whom were members of the more prosperous business class, he told them that Gibraltar 'is now considered throughout Europe as a Pest house,' and that this impression was bound to reduce the commerce going through the port.

Don's primary concern must have been for his garrison, however; he had the experience of Walcheren in the recent past, and Fort St. Philip at the start of his military career, to remind him how disease could cripple an army or a garrison far more severely than the guns of the enemy. So it is not surprising that the public health of Gibraltar became Don's first concern, and he wrote to Lord Bathurst, the Secretary of State for the Colonies.

> I began to perceive information relating to the fever, and having received from Medical persons and well informed inhabitants the most apposite and plausible opinions, some tending to prove it endemic, others epidemic, contagious and infectious, I have determined to consider it all four... I am myself without a doubt of the necessity of cleansing the Town of all the wretched Hovels which an overcrowded population has introduced, of opening out streets for the free circulation of air, and constructing proper drains. At present, were the inhabitants inclined to be cleanly, they are without the means of being so... I am afraid that it will be my lot to be under the painful necessity of reporting to your Lordship many unpleasant truths relative to the state of the Garrison and all the Departments in it...[4]

In this letter, Don also points out the need for a police force to enforce quarantine and any other of the health regulations which he proposed to institute. The voluntary civilian Inspectors of Health were impotent without a police to enforce improvements, and Don even considered imposing martial law to ensure that his decrees were carried out. Don's common-sense attitude to public health was the key to his success. If the rival theories of doctors could not let them agree on the measures to be taken to prevent an epidemic, then he would cover all the possibilities. This policy kept Gibraltar healthy for most of the many years that Don was in command, and his insistence on hygiene and slum clearance transformed the town into a far more salubrious place than it had been before his arrival.

Further reports continued to come in. The barracks were surveyed and many were found to be in a state of dilapidation. One of them, the Blue Barracks, was in a very poor condition. The Barrack Master remarked in his report that it had once been a hospital, and was perhaps more suited to this rôle (as a military hospital) once it had been repaired.

This idea must have appealed to Don. He would have known, from his earlier posting to Gibraltar, that the building, which in Spanish times had been a civilian hospital, had been used as the Army hospital in the previous century, even after the Naval Hospital had been built in the 1740s. He was concerned at the lack of hospital facilities for the soldiers of the garrison, who were not allowed to use the Naval Hospital and succeeded in taking over part of the Naval Hospital for the use of the Army. This arrangement was supposed to be temporary, until a Military Hospital could be built. But this hospital never materialized, and the Naval Hospital remained mainly for the use of soldiers.[5] The building now called Bleak House, when it was eventually built, was originally intended as a hospital, but was never used as one.

The idea of rebuilding the Blue Barracks as a hospital for the civilian population rather than for the garrison probably came to him then. The people of Gibraltar had lacked a hospital of their own for over a century. Shortly after the capture of Gibraltar in 1704, the *Hospital de la Santa Misericordia* (where the City Hall now stands) had become a prison, and the *Hospital de San Juan de Dios* had been converted into an Army Hospital, and then into the Blue Barracks. The Catholics now used a few rooms behind their church as a hospital, which retained the title of *Hospital de San Juan de Dios,* and the Jews and Protestants had similar arrangements, but these were totally inadequate, especially in times of epidemic. During the great epidemic of 1804, a temporary hospital had been built in Landport, just north of the city walls, and this was used for the civil inhabitants, but abandoned once the epidemic was over, and the funds raised for it were diverted to establish an

56

orphanage for the children of the thousands of victims of the epidemic.[6]

The richer civilian inhabitants were treated in their own homes by private physicians, who in Don's view were incompetent money-grubbers, while even some of the Garrison medical officers were involved in private practice 'which is detrimental to their regimental duties'. The poor, who could not afford the luxury of a private physician, often concealed their relatives who were suffering from the fever for fear of their being thrown into the common lazaretto; this delayed treatment and facilitated the spread of disease. A Civil Hospital was to be a key factor in Don's plans to prevent and control epidemics.

The troops had to be catered for too. Don made plans to build a Garrison Hospital, and in the interim, requested the use of the Naval Hospital for the use of soldiers. He had an acrimonious but brief disagreement with Admiral Fleming, who was in charge of the Naval establishment, over this, but with Lord Bathurst's support, he won the day. In the event, the Garrison Hospital was never built, and the Naval Hospital was subsequently devoted to the use of the troops, with sailors being admitted only by special request. In fact, the need for a large hospital for sailors had diminished dramatically with the end of the wars against Napoleon. In 1828, the Hospital was still referred to as the Military Hospital in the daily yellow fever returns published in the *Gibraltar Chronicle.*

Dr McMullen, an army physician who had served in the West Indies, and who therefore was well acquainted with the yellow fever, which periodically decimated the troops there, presented Don with a detailed report on the epidemic. His opinion that the disease was due to local causes (overcrowding and lack of sanitation) was incorrect, but it stimulated the improvements in the disposal of sewage which were to have such beneficial consequences for troops and civilians alike; but fortunately Don was too wise to reject out of hand the opposing theory of importation of the disease, and he kept the system of quarantine for ships in place.

A few days later, McMullen reported back to Don that the drains had been opened and cleaned, and plans for a system of sewers were being drawn up. The slaughterhouse and meat market, which was in a disgusting state, would be moved away from the town, and the disposal of sewage into the sea would be improved. The scavenging department was merely nominal and would have to be strengthened, so that filth could be removed from the streets every day. Officers of the Board of Health were to inspect the Town and South District to report on 'hovels' which should be demolished (this had been advised by the Board after the 1813 epidemic, but the recommendation had never been put into effect).

The Board also recommended that foreigners be prohibited from settling in Gibraltar without the Lieutenant Governor's permission, to prevent overcrowding and disease. In a letter to Lord Bathurst, Don described how the town had changed since his last posting in the 1790s: a shanty town of hovels and sheds now extended up the slope of the Rock above the town, and the houses in the town itself were now built to a height of three of four stories in order to accommodate the thousands of foreigners who had arrived in Gibraltar over the previous few years. He wrote that he would like to demolish all these sheds, but that there was no room to build elsewhere in order to accommodate the excess population. His conclusion to Lord Bathurst was that foreigners should be expelled, and the civilian population reduced to a maximum of 7000. He quotes the opinions of Governors Eliott and O'Hara, under whom he had served in Gibraltar, that the civilian population should not exceed six or seven thousand. The census of 1814 had shown that there were over 10,000 civilian inhabitants, and 'almost the whole Population of this Town is composed of Foreigners', who were a risk to security as well as to the public health, he insisted. Bathurst does not seem to have been receptive to this idea, and Don dropped the subject quietly, although he remained suspicious of the 'native' (i.e. non-British) inhabitants, 'a Class of People, who, while they pretend to the right, have not yet acquired the Sentiments of Englishmen,' and he felt strongly that it would be imprudent to try to establish any form of civil Government for them.

Because Don was anxious to thin out the population, and initially adhered strictly to the rules set out by Governor Bland in the previous century, which prohibited the grant of titles to properties to Catholic and Jewish inhabitants, he is often assumed to have been anti-Gibraltarian. But he felt that many properties had been acquired by foreign adventurers who had little long-term loyalty to Gibraltar, and who had made their money as privateers during the wars with France. He discriminated clearly, however, between those inhabitants whom he considered to be valuable citizens, and those of whom he disapproved, and his judgement was not only along religious or national lines. He classified the population as follows in a letter to Lord Bathurst:

1. Old established Mercantile Houses – 'generally composed of respectable people.'
2. Mercantile Adventurers, who were not accepted by commercial society, were numerous, troublesome, and connected with 'Pettifogging Attorneys', caused trouble between the garrison and the Inhabitants, and opposed most of the measures which he was attempting to introduce.
3. British shopkeepers and tradesmen (whom he considered just as troublesome as the Merchant Adventurers).
4. Foreign Shopkeepers and tradesmen he thought were not turbulent, and were easy to manage.
5. The Genoese – 'Many are rich; the poorer are Gardeners, Fishermen, Boatmen and Lightermen. They take advantage in Money transactions, but are not difficult to manage.'
6. Other inhabitants: Sicilians, Portuguese; 'a bad class of people.'
7. The old-established Jews were rich, and good subjects; the Barbary Jews were porters – 'a useful race of men,' but the hawkers and peddlers 'are a very bad set of people.' British Jews he found to be very refractory, and would not acknowledge the Head of the Jews as their representative. They insolently demanded 'what they call their rights as British Subjects.'
8. Of the Spaniards, he said 'Some are respectable' but in general they too were a source of nuisance.

Most of the second class, and all the lower orders of foreigners and Jews 'are dirty in their houses and their habits'. [7]

These letters were written shortly after he arrived in Gibraltar, and many of these opinions were no doubt influenced by reports from his Civil Secretary, John Stedman, his Military Secretary, Colonel Marshall, his Chief Medical Officer, WW Fraser, and others. But Don had been in Gibraltar before, and must have formed many of his impressions then. Certainly, his primary aim in seeking to deport as many 'foreigners' as possible was to relieve overcrowding and therefore the risk of further epidemics which might endanger the health of the Garrison.

Although Don felt strongly that the civil population of Gibraltar should not have a representative voice in Government, such as existed in Jersey, he nevertheless created many committees, for running different aspects of the administration, in which civilians were represented. The first was the Grand Jury, which he called for the first time in January 1815. He announced this to Bathurst in the same letter in which he delivers himself of the opinion on the Gibraltarians quoted in the previous paragraph. To be sure, this Grand Jury was convened only to agree to pay rates for the paving of the streets and refuse collection, and was composed exclusively of 'respectable British inhabitants,' but it was a start. He also tried to get the civilian inhabitants to agree to pay for the building of the Civil Hospital, but they must have jibbed at that, because he then appealed to Lord Bathurst for Crown money for this, as well as for the building of sewers and the public market, adding that the civil population would pay the running costs of the hospital.

> ... it is indispensably necessary that an Hospital for the Lower Classes of Civil Inhabitants should be established. I have selected for this object the Blue Barracks, which... will answer the purpose for the sick of the three persuasions viz. Protestants, Roman Catholics and Jews.
>
> As there is now not a moment to be lost in setting up the building as an Hospital, I have directed the repairs and alterations to be begun upon, and according to a rough estimate I feel the expence will amount to about three thousand pounds. Should your

Lordship disapprove of the measure, I beg you will acquaint me without delay, that I may stop the work...[8]

Don had a knack for 'creating facts', and fortunately Lord Bathurst did not seem to mind having his hand forced.

Not that his Lordship was a pushover in every case. He had not allowed Don to evict foreigners wholesale in order to thin out the population, and Don, accepting this, made arrangements for much of the population and the garrison to move to temporary dwellings in the Neutral Ground and the South during the fever season to relieve the overcrowding in the town. The experience of previous epidemics suggested that those who slept away from the town were less likely to contract the yellow fever, and a temporary township of huts in the isthmus had been used in the epidemics of 1813 and 1814. Don was happy to continue and extend this tried and proven scheme. Under his auspices, the village became an extensive planned suburb with one hundred wooden houses, separated by wide streets. They were easily removable, and occupied only from June to November. He ensured that a large part of the population moved there during the summer months to avoid overcrowding in the town, in order to reduce the possibility of contagion.

Although the village had been used in 1813, Don was careful to obtain at least local sanction from Spain for its further development. A joint proclamation with Lieutenant General Alós, the Commandant of the Campo area, on the 20th April 1815, stated that the Commandant at La Linea would provide help to British troops and inhabitants on the Neutral Ground, and permit the traffic of supplies during daytime hours.

In order to protect this village from storms, Don constructed a dike in Eastern Beach to prevent flooding during the winter storms, such as occurred in 1855.[9]

An important measure has been adopted to thin the dense population of the garrison during the summer months. In 1813, the erection of a village on the neutral ground was commenced, and under the auspices of Sir George Don, it has become an extensive suburb, consisting of about 100 wooden houses, laid

61

out in parallel and cross streets of ample width. The houses, or sheds, as they are called, are liable to be removed at the shortest notice, and they are occupied only between the 1st of June and the 1st of December annually...

....They have brick or wooden floors, which raise them about a foot from the soil. The foundations are of stone; the roofs are tiles or slates. The ventilation is good; every tenement having cross doors and windows, which admit of a thorough perflation, which is still further facilitated by their pointing either east or west, in the direction of the prevailing current of wind. Each house has one or more wells...

...Besides the regular houses, encampments have often been formed on the neutral ground. In 1819 the prevalence of an epidemic in Spain, as well as the plague in Barbary, rendered it necessary to establish a cordon of troops across the isthmus, and the town was thinned of several of the poorer inhabitants, consisting of Jews, Moors, &c. with their wives and families, to a number exceeding 500. They were encamped under the north front on raised platforms. [10]

Another problem, as Don saw it, was the poor quality of the civilian doctors:

'Fever... is aggravated by the professional ignorance of the Civil Medical Practitioners... their extreme ignorance and injurious mode of practice.'[11]

He convened a Medical Board to examine the qualifications of these doctors. Most of them refused to acknowledge the authority of the Board and ignored its requests for information. The diplomas and testimonials provided by the others were not considered to be of much value, as they were from Spain, where the level of medical training was considered inadequate by the British doctors.

... with the exception of a few individuals, the Civilian Medical Practitioners are little better than Empirics and consequently great mischief must ensue if such people are allowed to continue their avocation.

He felt, however, that he had no right to ban them from practice, in spite of their poor qualifications and failure to co-operate. However, he detailed several army surgeons to act as District Medical Officers, to look after the sick poor in their homes.

By June, his opinion of the civil population was rising. He praised

> ...the readiness evinced on the part of all classes of inhabitants to contribute by any means possible to the fulfilment of such objects, especially those considered to be connected with the public Health... the anxiety of the inhabitants to have the streets paved has induced them voluntarily to pay the assessed rate...[12]

On the 5th August 1815, the first wards of the Civil Hospital were opened to patients. The hospital was completed and officially opened by Don, as Governor of the hospital, in the presence of the three Deputy Governors (one from each of the three main religious denominations) and other dignitaries, in July 1816. This was reported in the *Gibraltar Chronicle:*[13]

> Two marble slabs, bearing the subjoined inscription, have been affixed by the Deputy Governors on the walls of the Hospital; and the elders of the Catholic Church have placed a full length Portrait of His Excellency the Lt. Governor in their Division of the Building.
>
> His Excellency General Don, Sir Charles Holloway, Commanding Royal Engineer, and the Representatives of the different Religious Persuasions, were pleased to express, in the strongest terms, their admiration of the unremitting zeal and ability of Mr Boschetti, by whose exertions an Edifice, comprising every advantage of convenience and utility, has arisen from the ruinous mass which formerly occupied the site.
>
> His Excellency General Don, at the same time expressed his high approbation of the great assiduity, and spirit of public zeal, evinced by the Deputy Governors, and the Medical Officers attached to the Establishment, in forwarding, by their united efforts, the object of the Institution, and in conferring on it the advantages of a well-regulated economy.
>
> Inscription.
>
> *In eternam Honorem Excellentissimi Georgii Don Exercitus Britannici Ducis Nec Non Munitionis Hujus Gibraltariae Praefecti Regii Sub Cujus Auspiciis Nosocomium Hoc Tripartitum in Usu Pauperum Imfirmorum Hujus Urbis Fundatum fuit Anno reparatae Salutis M. DCCC. XV. Monumentum Hoc Cives Gibraltarienses Posuerunt*

[The citizens of Gibraltar have erected this monument in eternal honour of the most excellent George Don, General of the British Army, and Commander of the Garrison of Gibraltar, under whose auspices this Triple Hospital for the use of the poor of this city was built in the year 1815].

One of these marble plaques can still be seen on the wall of the old St. Bernard's Hospital, the successor to George Don's Civil Hospital, which remained in use until 2005 as the general hospital for Gibraltar, when a new hospital, which was given the same name, was opened on reclaimed land in the Europort area.

The Catholic inhabitants had a full-length portrait of General Don painted and placed in their section of the hospital (it is now in the Gibraltar Museum). The division of the hospital into three almost independent parts by religion was to continue for well over half a century, until first the Catholic and Protestant wards, and then the Jewish ward, were amalgamated into what became the Colonial Hospital.

Don continued to support the hospital throughout his long custodianship of Gibraltar, and while he was in command he regularly attended the Annual Meetings, the proceedings of which were published in the *Gibraltar Chronicle.* At these meetings, he was always ready with words of praise and encouragement for the staff and the Deputy Governors.

Although the rebuilding of the hospital had been at the expense of the Crown, the running costs were not, and Don ordered that Port Dues should go to the hospital, as well as a tax on flour imposed on the bakers. Donations from wealthy Gibraltarians, and contributions from theatre performances helped to supplement this income.

Even such a worthy project as the hospital did not escape criticism. An anonymous letter, signed 'Britannicus,' was received by the Deputy Secretary for War, criticising Don bitterly for spending English public money on foreigners, and depriving the troops of much-needed barracks accommodation by building a hospital for civilians on the site of the Blue Barracks, and employing 'a Genoese Architect' (presumably Giovanni Maria Boschetti, who was in fact from Milan) and foreign labourers to boot![14]

Progress was also being made in the building of regimental hospitals, and a large hospital for the army on Europa Flats (it is now called Bleak House):[15]

> On Europa Flats, Sir George Don has erected a very handsome hospital, of lofty, cool and capacious wards, intended as a reserve against the breaking out of any dangerous fever; where the sick may be nursed without the least fear of infecting the other parts of the rock....

Since he had already obtained the use of the Naval Hospital, it reained a 'reserve hospital', for use in epidemics. In 1825 it was converted into accommodation for officers of the 42nd Regiment, which had just arrived on the Rock.[16] Don had ordered moveable temporary hospitals for the troops, and when these hospitals arrived, they would be converted into summer barracks for the troops once the regimental hospitals were built.

Yellow fever was not the only concern in Don's mind. In November, a proclamation by the Lieutenant Governor announced the introduction of vaccination against smallpox. This was not to be compulsory, but it was free, although each subject had to pay one dollar, to induce them to return for a second visit when it could be confirmed that the vaccination had been successful, when the dollar would be refunded. Gibraltar had in fact been one of the first places outside Britain where Jennerian vaccination had been used, when Drs Marshall and Walker sailed from England in 1800 on a mission to spread vaccination throughout Europe. With the permission of the Governor, General O'Hara, they vaccinated all the susceptible soldiers in the Garrison.[17]

In 1816 another threat loomed on the horizon. Bubonic plague began to spread across the Mediterranean from the east, brought back by Muslim pilgrims returning from the Haj, and it established itself in Morocco in 1817, where hundreds were dying every day. Energetic quarantine measures by Don and his Spanish counterpart, the Governor of the Campo area, General José María Alós, prevented its spread across the Straits, and probably saved

Europe from another Black Death. Don provided four Quarantine Guard vessels to patrol the Straits and the Bay, and men in rowing boats, who patrolled the coast at night. On the Spanish side, General Alós situated a cordon of soldiers along nineteen leagues of the coastline on either side of the Rock. Don and Alós were in daily communication, and Don was in personal contact with correspondents in every coastal town and village between Cádiz and Málaga. He put stringent restrictions on communication with ships in the Bay, and limited all communication with Tangier to the 'Quarantine Schooner', the *Pacífico,* which carried essential mail, which had to be fumigated before being distributed. A proclamation by Don on 13th June 1818, printed in the *Gibraltar Chronicle,* states starkly that those introducing any sort of goods from a ship in quarantine would be 'Guilty of felony, and liable to the punishment of death.' There do not seem to have been any executions, in Gibraltar at least, for this offence: perhaps the threat alone was enough of a deterrent.

At the same time, there was another epidemic of yellow fever in Spain, but under Don's watchful eye, Gibraltar remained free of any major epidemic until 1828.

Don had been quick to take note of the abominable state of the drains in Gibraltar, and the dirty, pitted streets, where foul matter was allowed to rot in the potholes; also there were 'depôts' around the town where filth was piled up to be removed at leisure by the single, poorly paid scavenger who was evidently quite unequal to the job. This was another obvious cause of disease. He wrote to Bathurst on November 29, 1814: [18]

> ...notwithstanding every effort in my power for the last four weeks, the Town and even the South District are still in a very filthy state, I however hope by further arrangements which I have just made that in the course of two months I may be able to effect a thorough cleansing of the whole fortress.
>
> In my ride today I observed, that the streets were completely broken up, and deep ruts formed, which become receptacles for dirt; the new paving of the streets will therefore be one of the first objects of my attention.

The action which he had taken was to convene a Grand Jury composed of civil inhabitants to decide on a plan for financing the paving and cleaning of the streets, and the building of a sewerage system. The Grand Jury met in January 1815, and no doubt prompted by Don, agreed that householders would pay a yearly rate (3%) for this purpose. This was unprecedented, but it seems to have been accepted by the Gibraltarians without much fuss. The sewers were designed by the Royal Engineers, and built rapidly, and a Committee for Paving and Scavenging was set up which administered the rates collected.

This committee was composed of both civilians and government officials, but the civilians were in a majority. Lighting the town was added to the duties of this committee later, and an extra one third of one per cent was added to the rates for this purpose. The construction of a system of sewers had been recommended by a previous Grand Jury, which had been convened a decade earlier after the great yellow fever epidemic of 1804; but no action had been taken since then, either on this, or on the improvements to the system of scavenging which had been recommended at the same time.

The new sewers were a great improvement on the almost total lack of hygiene in Gibraltar prior to 1814.[19]

It appears, that previous to the year 1814, there were very few drains in Gibraltar; and for want of them, large accumulations of filth called <u>dirt's depôts</u> were established in various parts of the town. In 1815, the reconstruction of the drains took place, and, since that time, they have been continued at various periods up the hillside; and the gullies have been covered, which undoubtedly is an improvement in the state of the drains.

But they were by no means perfect, and even after they were improved on Don's orders after the yellow fever epidemic of 1828, the stench of sewage, especially in the summer, was often overpowering.[20]

From some cause or other, the sewers emit, in the summer months, a most foetid smell; this mephitic odour, no doubt, proceeds from causes which may be removed. In the summer of 1844, the stench along the line wall was intolerable, and silver articles, belonging

67

to persons living in houses in this locality were almost entirely blackened, evidently from the quantity of sulphuretted hydrogen gas composing the effluvia from the sewers which open into the sea near this locality.

Kelaart, who was a medical man himself, had no doubt about the basic soundness of the sewers constructed under General Don, because he adds that he has not the least doubt that the improvements in the sewers could only be followed by an improvement in the health of the Garrison: 'Long will the boon conferred upon the inhabitants by the late General Don be remembered.'

The markets were another cause for concern. The slaughterhouse and meat market was cramped, dilapidated and unventilated, and was situated in the centre of the town. It was without water or drainage, was consequently foul-smelling, and was judged by Don to be 'a public nuisance, and injurious to the health of the Inhabitants during the summer months.' He ordered a new market to be built in the Neutral Ground, not far from the Devil's Tower, and well away from the houses of the town, and paid for it out of Crown revenues. The fish market was provided with a well and drainage to help in keeping it clean.

Lack of water, especially in the summer, was another perennial health problem. Gibraltar had no assured supply of water, apart a few wells, many of them supplying uncertain amounts of rather brackish water. Finding large channels of rainwater around St. Michael's Cave, he arranged for these to be diverted into a lake in the cave, from where it would filter down towards the aqueduct. Wells were dug in the Neutral Ground, both to supply the summer village and for shipping, as well as for watering the extensive vegetable gardens there. In 1818, during a period of drought, he ordered more wells to be dug, and in 1825, during another dry season, extra water tanks were built near Jumper's Bastion. Within the town, Don ordered that all new houses should be built with a cistern for the purpose of collecting rain-water, to make each house as self-sufficient for water as possible.

Water was formerly an article scarce and expensive in this garrison. But since 1814, every house which has been built has had a tank constructed in it. The number of these tanks, which now amount to about 250 or 300, affords a supply of tolerably good water... but the poorer classes have seldom access to those tanks, and must purchase water obtained from wells in the garrison, or on the Neutral Ground, which, at the latter part of the summer, is frequently thick and muddy, and at all times rather brackish. [21]

Many years later, the Water Catchments were to be constructed on the eastern slopes of the Rock as a means of supplying the whole population with potable water. These catchments have now been dismantled, as desalination now meets the bulk of Gibraltar's requirements, but many houses in Gibraltar still receive a significant supply of their fresh water from the cisterns built underneath them, a long enduring benefit which derives from the foresight of General George Don.

NOTES

1. Don to Bathurst. 29 Oct. 1814. Governors Letters, GGA.
2. Sweetland, *Report on the Trade of Gibraltar*. 26 Nov. 1829. Governors Letter Books. GGA.
3. Benady, S. pp 74-88.
4. Don to Bathurst. 29 Oct. 1814. Governors Letters, GGA.
5. Lawrance, p. 47.
6. Account book of Board of Health, 1804. GGA.
7. Public Records Office: CO 91/61, 91/63.
8. Don to Bathurst. 20 March 1815. Governors Letters, GGA.
9. Montero, p. 26.
10. Hennen, p 72.
11. Don to Bathurst. 4 May 1815. Governors Letters, GGA.
12. Don to Bathurst. 21 June 1815. ibid..
13. Gibraltar Chronicle. 17 July 1816. ibid.
14. Public Records Office: CO 91/68.
15. Beauclerk, p 319.
16. Anton, p 334.
13. Don to Bathurst. 29 Nov. 1814. Governors Letters, GGA.
14. Amiel, p 2.
15. Kelaart, pp 33-34..

16. Don to Bathurst. 26 Dec. 1814. Governors Letters, GGA.
17. Bailey, p 22.
18. Hennen, p 16.
19. Don to Bathurst. 22 Sept. 1825. Governors Letters, GGA. Hennen, pp 23-24; Rey HJ-M, p 12; Anton, p 345.
20. Kelaart, p 32.
21. Amiel, p 1.

Miniature painting of Don as a young man.
(courtesy of the Anderson Collection).

Portrait of Don.
(Oil painting, Queen Elizabeth Castle, Jersey).

The Duc de Crillon, victor at Minorca, shown riding triumphantly over the Rock (which he failed to capture).
(From an 18th century Spanish print).

Lieutenant General the Hon. James Murray, the defender of Fort St. Philip
(*From a print dated ca. 1773*)

Portrait of General Don.
(Mezzotint by Samuel Reynolds, 1808, after C G Dillon)

Portrait of General Don. Presented by the Catholic Inhabitants to the Civil Hospital, Gibraltar. *(Gibraltar Museum)*

Sketch of General Don by Capt Henderson, ca. 1803
(from a Ms. in the Gibraltar Garrison Library)

Statue of General Don in Royal Parade, St. Helier, Jersey
(Photo: S. Benady)

Coat of Arms of the Don family.
(Charter of Arms, 1810, in Anderson Collection)

The Convent; Residence of the Governor of Gibraltar
(From an old postcard, ca. 1910)

Governor's Cottage, Gibraltar
(From a postcard, ca. 1910)

San Felipe Street, San Roque.
(From an albumen print, ca. 1870)

The Civil Hospital, As it was after reconstruction in 1882.
(From an old postcard)

Monument to the Duke of Wellington, Alameda Botanic Gardens, Gibraltar.
From a postcard ca. 1920.

The Don Gates, Alameda Botanic Gardens.
(Photo: S Benady)

Marble plaque commemorating the opening of the Civil Hospital,
Gibraltar, in 1815.

Bust of General Don, Exchange
Building, Gibraltar.
(Photo: Slim Simpson)

Monument to Don,
Cathedral of the Holy
Trinity, Gibraltar.

Monuments to Lady Don and her sister, Ann Murray.
English Cemetery, Piazza Donatello, Florence.

Chapter 7

THE ALAMEDA, ROADS AND AGRICULTURE.

Don's preoccupation with the welfare of the garrison and the inhabitants of Gibraltar extended far beyond a mere concern for their physical health. His initial inspections of Gibraltar, both within the walls and outside, would have shown him a dirty, overcrowded and dilapidated town, and to the south of it, a desert of red sand, which had long been used as a burial ground. These sands surrounded the main parade ground, Grand Parade, which had been laid out in 1756, on the orders of the Governor, Lord Tyrawley, by his son, Captain Charles O'Hara, who later also became a Governor of Gibraltar, and Captain Rainsford. This Parade was where the troops had assembled before the Great Sortie in 1781.

By March 1815 George Don had already formulated plans for turning this desert into a garden for the benefit of the community, and had given this projected pleasure garden a name the 'New Alameda,' - the Alameda up till then had been the name given to the main square of the town (now John Mackintosh Square). On March 19th [1] he ordered that excess money from the rates collected for the sewers should be set aside for this new project. But much more money would be required. He judged that Lord Bathurst, who had coughed up Crown money for the building of the Civil Hospital, was not likely to be so receptive to the idea of financing this project, and although Don had got away with charging householders a yearly rate for paving and scavenging: he knew that he would probably face a riot if he tried to impose another rate - and for something not so obviously necessary as a public garden, at that.

He must have turned his mind back to his experience as Lieutenant Governor of Jersey for the solution to this problem. There, unable to get Whitehall to finance his plans to develop the road system, even though it was a military necessity, he had successfully raised money by a public lottery. Why not do the same in Gibraltar?

To think was to act. The first lottery was drawn in June 1815. Three more followed in 1816, and one each in 1817 and 1818

71

and two in 1820, and the Alameda was progressively improved and extended, from a simple circle of walks around the Grand Parade, to a more elaborate pleasure garden with shady trees, shrubberies, bandstands and summerhouses.

In December 1815, he must have decided to try Lord Bathurst's patience after all, and he chose a project which he felt might appeal to London, by linking it to General Eliott, the hero of the Great Siege.

I beg leave to acquaint your Lordship that from there being no place of public recreation in this Garrison, I was induced last summer to establish a walk around the Grand Parade, and form what is called in this country an Alameda, where the Inhabitants might enjoy the air protected from the extreme heat of the sun; careful that no expense should be occasioned to His Majesty's Government, I obtained from a contribution of the Amateur Theatre *and other means* [my italics] the funds necessary for the undertaking; the walks are now nearly completed, with shrubberies round them, and this seems to have afforded such general satisfaction that I am anxious a summer House or Rotunda should be built on a rising ground on the South side of the Grand Parade which commands a most extensive view in almost every direction.

I take the liberty of laying before your Lordship a plan of the Rotunda, and as Marble can be procured from Carrara at as cheap a rate as cut stone, it is intended, that this building should be constructed of that material.

The Grand Parade was founded by General Eliott, and as there is no public Monument to his memory in the Garrison, I feel extremely desirous, that a statue of him should be placed upon the Rotunda, and I trust when your Lordship calls to mind the circumstances of the Siege of 1782, that you will concur with me in opinion, that a work which might commemorate on the spot the conduct of this distinguished man, would in affording an honorable tribute to his name, give the best incentive to an imitation of his actions.

May I hope from what I have stated your Lordship will pardon my requesting you to countenance a Subscription towards raising sufficient funds for purchasing a colossal statue of the late General Eliott, and also in aid of defraying the cost of the Rotunda, in which it is to be placed. [2]

72

Don was careful to keep Whitehall in the dark about the lotteries, although in fact these were legal in Britain at the time; he never mentioned them in his despatches to London, and he continued to keep his superiors in Whitehall in the dark to the end (see below). On this occasion, he was unsuccessful in getting money out of Bathurst, and the proposed marble Rotunda was not built; the original statue of Eliott which he placed in the Gardens stood in a raised circle of stone. It was a wooden statue, which was carved locally out of the bowsprit of the Spanish man of war, *San Juan*, which had been captured at Trafalgar, and which had been Don's first lodging in Gibraltar. This statue now stands in the Convent, having been replaced much later (in 1853) by the bronze bust set on a column which now stands in the Alameda.

The Alameda was formally opened to the public in April 14th 1816, with three brass bands in attendance, but the improvements and extensions continued for years after. It was quite true that money collected for the performances of the amateur theatre groups was of some help towards the upkeep of the Gardens, but their contribution was quite small compared to the amount collected from the lotteries.

In 1820, Don was responsible for placing another monument in the Alameda; this time it was a bust of the Duke of Wellington. On this occasion he did not even approach Bathurst for funds. The money was raised by a 'voluntary' contribution of a day's pay, which was deducted from the pay of civil and military officers and all other ranks. The bust, which had been cast from bronze taken from French guns which had been captured by the Iron Duke himself, was placed on a Roman column brought from the ruins of Leptis Magna ('Lepida' on the inscription), and donated to the Lieutenant Governor by Richard Turner, captain of HM Supply ship *Weymouth*.[3] The rest of the cargo of Roman antiquities, which had been donated by the Pasha of Lebida to the Prince Regent, can still be seen in England, in Virginia Water.

In later years George Don found another source of income for the Alameda: he sold the exclusive agency for the sale of Spanish Lottery tickets to the highest bidder. This enterprise eventually came to the ears of Whitehall, and on 3rd August 1829, we find Sir George Don replying to an enquiry from Sir George Murray, who had succeeded Lord Bathurst as the Secretary of State for the Colonies:

> In 1815 I considered it very desireable that an Alameda should be formed to induce the troops and the Inhabitants to take walking exercise and accordingly pleasure grounds were laid out and planted, and Bridges, and Summer houses were constructed. The expenses incurred in this work were defrayed by voluntary subscriptions (the inhabitants being then opulent and trade prosperous) and from the proceeds of Balls, Plays, Concerts, public amusements etc.

Again Don was careful not to mention his own lotteries, but with more reason this time: lotteries had just been made illegal in Britain.

He protested that the money raised had been used only in 'support of the public Alameda', that the concession scrupulously fair, being given always to the highest bidder, but he added that if Murray still insisted, he would terminate the practice 'but I must observe that the measure will deprive us of one of the means of supporting the Alameda, and the Troops and Inhabitants of an agreeable resource.'[4]

It was all to no avail; Murray was not to be moved. On January 1830, General Don, ironically, was the signatory to a proclamation banning all lotteries in Gibraltar.

In September 1830, Boisson, the Editor of the *Gibraltar Chronicle* since its inception in 1801, who had acted as treasurer of the fund for 15 years, retired, giving way to George White, the Civil Secretary. There was a deficit, and Sir George Don, typically, made it up himself with a donation of $396 (This was the Spanish dollar, current in Gibraltar, and worth just over 4 shillings).

But the Alameda continued to thrive, and attracted many favourable comments from visitors over the years. Beauclerk, writing in 1828, gives perhaps the most vivid picture of the gardens as they were in George Don's time.[5]

> To the South of the town, lie the public gardens or Alameda, of considerable extent, and exquisite beauty. The softness of the climate of Gibraltar is such, that the trees are barely three months

74

deprived of their foliage, the varied brilliancy of which produces a most enchanting coup d'oeil. Two Chinese pavilions are placed at convenient distances, affording retirement from the heat of the sun; and sentries are posted at various points, to prevent any mutilation of the trees or flowers by the public, who are allowed to wander about the gardens unmolested. Marble seats and rustic chairs of uneasy-notoriety, beneath the thick shade of a species of white maple, are everywhere found to be tenanted by hard sitters...

The walks, and geranium hedges, are kept in the greatest order, and an extensive parade ground, surrounded by walks and trees, spread over a level space... Below this military grid-iron, a few green fields slope easily down to the sea-lines of the fortifications. But a few years since, these beautiful gardens were not in being; a barren waste of sand and rock occupied their present situation. Two well-macadamised roads lead you to the southern parts of the rock, both shaded by overhanging trees...

As Beauclerk noted, the two roads which led to the South District (Rosia Road and Europa Road) were constructed at the same time as the Alameda Gardens. Roads were also built on Europa Flats, making that area much more accessible, and another author [6] remarks that Don built roads on the Upper Rock, which made it possible for the first time to ride on horseback to the summit, and that 'the whole Rock of Gibraltar is intersected by roads, broad and smooth, all adapted for horse exercise, and most of them for carriages.' Indeed, Disraeli mentions that Sir George himself rode up to St. Michael's Cave in a four-horse carriage.[7]

In addition to constructing roads to all parts of the Rock, Don planted trees along them to provide much-needed shade in the summer. Kelaart[8] writes that Don introduced the Bellasombra to Gibraltar, 'one of the many foreign plants introduced into Gibraltar by Sir George Don.' Many of these plants went into the Alameda, but others must have been planted in the Convent garden, under the watchful eye of Lady Don. Elsewhere, the same author comments:

I am sure if General Don's plan was still further carried out, by planting more poplars, firs and *bellasombras* on the higher parts of the rock, Gibraltar might be rendered a cooler residence in the course of years.

Roads within the town were extended and repaired, and it was even possible to run a stage coach service between the South District and the town:[9]

By the unwearied exertions of Sir George Don, the roads and communications are now so improved and extended, that wheel-carriages can proceed to almost every point of the rock; and private vehicles of this description, for the purposes of luxury, which were scarcely known before 1814, now abound. Public carriages can also be hired, and even a stage-coach has been established, which plies between the south and the town regularly during the summer months. A great number of foot roads, ramps, and flights of steps have been constructed, by which the access to the habitations of the lower orders, on the hill-side, has been greatly improved, and the facilities for removing filth increased to a very considerable degree.

George Don's zeal for improving communications was not confined to Gibraltar. Shortly after his arrival in December 1814 he was already arranging to build a road along the Neutral Ground to meet another which was being constructed between San Roque and Gibraltar by Lieutenant General Alós, the Spanish Commandant of the Campo de Gibraltar.

Apart from the road to San Roque, Don built other roads in Spain, and set up a fund which was subscribed by inhabitants and officers alike, for building and maintaining the roads in the Campo area.

But Gibraltar is a limited theatre for his Excellency, and he has civilised Spain for twenty miles round, by making roads at his own expense, building bridges, and reforming posadas.[10] There are no roads [in the Campo de Gibraltar], properly so called, within the vicinity, excepting those at Gibraltar, and that which the Governor has made to San Roque, his usual residence. Formerly the latter was impassable to a carriage, as is now the mule-path to Algesiras.[11]

Ten years later, the road system in the Campo de Gibraltar had been expanded. In March 1828, the *Gibraltar Chronicle* printed the accounts of 'Expences incurred in repairing the roads from Gibraltar to San Roque, Venta del Carmen, Almoraima etc.' There

76

was a deficit of nearly $400 (about £85), and of course, there was a donation by Sir George of the identical amount to cover it.

This improvement in the roads of the area allowed a stage-coach to run between Gibraltar and San Roque. While there is no doubt that the good roads were to the benefit of the officers who rode in the Royal Calpe Hunt, and to Sir George, who made the journey to his house in San Roque in comfort as a result, Don's programme of road maintenance must have been of incalculable benefit to the Spanish inhabitants of the Campo, both by improving communications and by providing them with jobs on road construction.

> The late Sir George Don, whilst Lieut Governor of the Fortress, invariably passed several months of the year in San Roque; and his noble hospitality, his ever open purse, and constant employment of the poor in works of utility, secured him the love and respect of all classes of its inhabitants. Indeed, such was the gallant Veteran's influence in this place, that I may literally say, not a stone could be turned nor a tree planted without ``His Excellency's'' being first consulted as to the propriety of the measure.[12]

The other great garden in Gibraltar was the garden of the Convent - the Governor's residence - and Maria Don seems to have been responsible for its development; many visitors to Gibraltar remarked on the beauties to be seen there in the garden which she had embellished:

> ...the Government House, is an old convent, and one of the most delightful residences I know, with a garden under the superintendence of Lady Don, full of rare exotics, with a beautiful terrace over the sea, a berceau of vines, and other delicacies which would quite delight you.[13]

Richard Ford, writing in the 1840s, has this to say:

> It [the Convent] is a good residence. The garden, so nicely laid out by Lady Don, used to be delicious. Scotch horticulture under an Andalusian climate can wheedle anything out of Flora and Pomona...'[14]

This last quotation, referring to the Scottish origin of the Dons, also suggests that, little more than a decade after Maria Don left the Convent, it had been allowed to deteriorate.

77

Who can doubt that Mrs Don, as she then was, must also have played an important part in the decision to create the Alameda Gardens, and in the planning that went into making them the success that they became? In fact, there is some evidence for this - a pen and ink sketch by Major General Henry Sandham, executed in the 1820s, shows a scene from the Alameda Gardens, entitled; 'Alameda, Lady Don's Garden.'[15]

It was only to be expected that Don, who had established a farm in Jersey in order to provide vegetables for the population, should not have had similar concerns in Gibraltar, which was almost totally dependent on imports of foodstuffs from Spain or Morocco, which would almost inevitably be cut off in time of war. As early as December 1814, he was requesting a plough and harrier 'for the Lieutenant Governor's Garden.'[16] This garden was in the Neutral Ground, to the north of the Governor's Meadow, which itself bordered on the Inundation (Laguna). It was one of the vegetable gardens by North Front which had been long established. Don encouraged and extended these, and had wells dug in order to supply them with water. He ordered the rubbish which was collected by the Scavenging Department in the town to be transported to the gardens for use as fertilizer.[17]

> …we came upon the Neutral Ground, which is sandy and quite barren, except for a tract of a few acres, where the present governor has made a garden for the supply of the garrison. This spot has been manured by the sweepings of the streets, reduced to ashes, and produces a variety of herbs for the market. Here are the houses of the gardeners, which with the large wheels for raising water turned by mules, the unknown vegetables cultivated in some of the fields, and the inclosures made by the woven canes, or of a shrub with immense leaves shaped like that of a tulip, offered many picturesque little scenes.[18]

He also toyed with the idea of covering Europa Flats with earth and manure, in order to establish a vegetable farm there, but was apparently dissuaded by his officers, who thought that this might facilitate a possible landing of an invading force, by providing it with cover.[19] In fact, the real reason for Don giving up on this idea must

78

have been that he realised that Europa Flats were far too windswept and exposed for such a project to have any chance of success.

An American visitor to Gibraltar in 1818 was impressed with the appearance of Gibraltar, and the extent of vegetable growing which had been achieved: [20]

> The town is very pleasant, for English industry and wealth have made it so in defiance of nature. I have seen few towns of the same size more neat or more comfortable, and, what is yet more extraordinary, still fewer that have so many or so fine gardens. Indeed, a general horticulture has been carried so far under the present excellent governor, that, instead of depending on the neighbouring villages, Gibraltar exports to them different kinds of vegetables throughout the whole year.

It seems unlikely, although by no means impossible, that this last statement is correct, and that there was any significant export of foodstuffs from Gibraltar.

NOTES

1. Military Secretary's Letters. 29th March 1816. GGA.
2. Don to Bathurst. Governor's Letters 26th Dec. 1815. GGA.
3. Gwyther Jones.
4. Don to Murray. Governor's Letters, 3rd Aug. 1829. GGA. (This was General Sir George Murray who, as far as I can tell, was no relation to Lady Don).
5. Beauclerk.
6. Inglis, Vol I, p 42; Vol III p 161.
7. Disraeli, R. (ed), p 24.
8. Kelaart, p 145.
9. Hennen, p 65.
10. Disraeli, R (ed), p 9.
11. Anon (1), p.13
12. Rochfort Scott, pp. 43-44.
13. Disraeli,R, *op. cit.* pp. 8-9.
14. Ford, R. (1966 edition, Vol II, p. 513).
15. C Finlayson (ed). p 91.
16. Military Secretary's Letters, 7th December 1814. GGA.
17. Military Secretary's Letters, 19th May 1926. GGA.
18. Anon (1). p. 33.

19. Beauclerk, p. 318; Ford, p. 518.
20. Ticknor, Vol I, p. 236.

Chapter 8

BUILDINGS AND INSTITUTIONS.

It cannot be said that George Don rebuilt Gibraltar; no doubt he would have wished to do so, but lack of funds must have inhibited even him, and the nature of the terrain dictates that to this day the basic town plan of the old City is not very different from what it was in the 17th Century.[1] His sense of order was reflected in the regular plan of the 'Summer Village' in the Neutral Ground, where 'under the auspices of Sir George Don [the village] has become an extensive suburb, consisting of about 1000 wooden houses, laid out in parallel and cross streets of ample width.'[2]

However, by among other things clearing slums, establishing a sewage system, and repairing road surfaces and developing the road system outside the town, he transformed the town of Gibraltar from a disease-ridden rabbit warren, which had not been rebuilt to any great extent since the ravages of the Great Siege of the previous century, into a relatively more salubrious home for the Gibraltarians, although the poor still had to live in overcrowded squalor on the upper areas of the town for many years after his time.

Upon the whole, although Gibraltar is improved to a degree scarcely to have been contemplated by those who knew it before his Excellency Sir George Don took the command, it is even now a town, in many parts of it, confined and ill ventilated, in which innumerable obstacles to cleanliness exist, and with a population, filthy in themselves, and over-crowded, perhaps, beyond any other community in the world.[3]

Apart from the direct initiatives of Sir George Don, there were two factors which stimulated the rebuilding of the town of Gibraltar: the first was the increase in commerce and the consequent prosperity in the early years of his command, and the second was Don's action, at Whitehall's behest, and after some initial resistance on his part because of his poor opinion of certain sectors of the population, in setting up a committee to decide on the titles to property in Gibraltar, which up until then had been governed by rules set up

81

by Governor Bland in the previous century, which only allowed British Protestants to own property. These rules were regularly flouted, so that the titles to most buildings were legally dubious, to say the least.

Once their titles had been confirmed under the new system, the inhabitants would have been far less reluctant to rebuild their houses or effect improvements than they had been under the previous ambiguous system, where a Catholic or Jewish householder was liable to be dispossessed if the letter of the previous law were to be upheld, and even a British Protestant house-owner's title was in jeopardy if he had acquired his property from a Jew or a Roman Catholic.

Commercial Gibraltar; The Exchange and Commercial Library.

Gibraltar had enjoyed an unprecedented prosperity during the wars with France which culminated in the Battle of Waterloo in 1815. The blockades imposed by the warring parties allowed a flourishing entrepôt trade through Gibraltar. Even after 1815, the boom lasted for years. John Sweetland, the Captain of the Port, in his paper for Don on the trade of Gibraltar, had this comment to make:

> The question may be said to stand thus - A fair has been held in Gibraltar which lasted from 1806 to 1826, a period of twenty years. That fair is now ended, yet Gibraltar is not ruined, it is still a Bazaar, where strangers find every sort of commodity...[4]

Under these circumstances, it was natural that the commercial class in Gibraltar should aspire to be more than just a barely tolerated appendage of the garrison. In 1806, some of the merchants, piqued at the refusal of the officers of the Garrison to allow them to be members of the Garrison Library, had founded the Commercial Library for their own use, and some local merchants, like John Arengo and Aaron Cardozo, built themselves lavish homes.

In 1818, General Don opened the New Exchange building, the construction of which he had inspired and encouraged. He would have taken note of the remarks of the Grand Jury which he had convened in 1815 about the inadequacy of the existing Auction Room. The building was designed by Don's Chief Engineer, Major General Sir Charles Holloway. Don's address at the opening praised

82

the traders and the spirit of co-operation which now reigned among them:[5]

> The result, Gentlemen, we now see: We possess, in this fabric, a Public Exchange, and Auction Mart, of a simple but monumental exterior, massive and durable in its construction, and commodious in the distribution of its offices and apartments, where, if the conveniences of business have been studied, the means of literary resources, and of recreation, have not been neglected.

In reply, the Chairman, Mr Duguid, paid tribute to help and support in the creation of the Exchange, and dwelt also on the many benefits which Don had brought to the inhabitants of Gibraltar. The Exchange building would also house the Commercial Library, which had already been in existence for some years.

Above the main gate which Don had unlocked in opening the New Exchange, the merchants of Gibraltar placed a bust of Don, recording that it had been paid for by public subscription. This bust, which can still be seen on the Main Street façade of the building, which is now the House of Assembly, is inscribed 'George Don', which might be taken to imply that it was placed there before 1819, when Don finally received his GCB. It is unlikely, though, that it was there when the building was inaugurated, which would have been an unprecedented tribute to a living Lieutenant Governor, and as it is dedicated 'in Grateful Remembrance of His Paternal Government', it is likely that it was put there after his death. It is mentioned by 1844 [6]. The Gibraltar Chronicle (4th March 1879) confirms that the bust dates from years after the inauguration of the building; an article in it about the proposal to erect a statue of Don in Jersey, records that the bust of Don in the Exchange had been placed by the inhabitants 'several years ago.'

Titles to Property

Property owning in Gibraltar had hitherto been governed by the rules laid down by Governor Humphrey Bland in the middle of the previous century. Then the aim had been to populate the Rock with British Protestants, whose loyalty to the crown was considered to be guaranteed. Only they were to be allowed to own property; Catholics and Jews could not. Over the years, this law had been bypassed time and time again. Even Governor Bland himself did not adhere strictly to the letter of his own law. Many properties were in fact owned by Catholics or Jews, with a Protestant inhabitant merely supplying the name which appeared in the deeds.

Don fully approved of Bland's system, which allowed only British Protestants to own land, and viewed its implementation as an essential means to deter 'foreigners' from settling permanently in the already over-populated town of Gibraltar, adding to the overcrowding which he believed was a security as well as a health risk. He considered that too many properties had been bought by foreigners who had made their fortunes out of privateering during the war against Napoleon, and that these individuals had little or no loyalty or commitment to the British Crown, or to Gibraltar.

He disapproved strongly of the custom, instituted in the previous decade by Lieutenant Governor Trigge and others, of allowing Catholics and Jews to own property if they had been resident in Gibraltar for a mere five years, although he thought that it would be unreasonable to rescind the titles to properties which had been in the hands of Catholics or Jews for many years. He recommended to Whitehall that in future Catholics and Jews *should* be permitted to own property, but only provided they had become British subjects by residential qualification – he originally suggested a minimum period of fifteen years. But by the time that the Order in Council of 1817 was published, which provided for the fifteen-year residence qualification which he had demanded, he now believed that this was too short, although he had suggested it only a year earlier.

As commander of the garrison he felt that such 'liberalisation' was likely to be a security risk, but by 1817, when Whitehall had determined to legalise the ownership of property by Catholics and Jews, he had come to understand the local population better, and was on good terms with some of the wealthy merchants. He was therefore quite willing to create a Commission for the investigation of titles to lands, and when the local property-holders formed a committee to argue the matter, he was prepared to meet with them, and to consider their arguments. He warned them against the terms of the Memorial that they wished to send to the Prince

84

Regent requesting the revocation of the Order, and refused to pass it on. He made it clear that he would oppose revocation of Bland's rules, but he was prepared to listen to grievances.

The Committee persisted, and sent a deputation to London, consisting of James Oxberry, Charles Glyn, with Aaron Cardozo as spokesman, asking, among other things, for a reduction of the residential qualification to seven years. After much deliberation, the Order in Council was amended, but the period of residence required remained at fifteen years, which can have pleased neither Don nor the memorialists. It is not surprising therefore, that when Aaron Cardozo published in 1830 the testimonials and letters of recommendation which he had solicited and received, from 1818 onwards, from eminent friends and acquaintances from the Duke of Kent downwards, there was no contribution from General Don.[7]

The Commissioners for Settling the Titles to Lands, to give them their full title, were all British Protestant civilian inhabitants or Army officers, but they seem to have carried out their work thoroughly and impartially. They requested all those claiming properties to come to them with their claims, which were all published in supplements to the *Gibraltar Chronicle* over several years. By the time they had finished, all the properties in Gibraltar had been assigned to their proper owners, and the fiction that they were all owned by British Protestants had finally been laid to rest.

Charters of Justice and the Court-House

In 1817, Gibraltar received its fourth Charter, which established Courts of Civil Pleas, Appeal, General Sessions, Quarter Sessions and Petty Sessions. For the first time Gibraltar had a legally qualified civilian judge, who sat with Don to try criminal cases, and with two civilian inhabitants to try civil cases. Prior to this, Don had complained to Whitehall that the Court House was in a ruinous state, and asked permission to overhaul it completely: [8]

> Until my arrival here all the public buildings only underwent what is called necessary and temporary repairs, a system which has been productive of great and constant inconvenience to the troops and an enormous expense to the public.

The Court House was duly rebuilt, and the result was the building which is still in use today.

Towards the end of Don's time, the Fifth Charter of Justice in 1830 established a Supreme Court to try civil and criminal cases, and a Supreme Court Judge was appointed, who sat with a Jury for criminal cases, and with civilian assessors in civil cases. The Governor no longer tried cases, and the foundation of Gibraltar's present legal system was laid. Don (Gibraltar Chronicle, October 26th 1830) remarked at the reading of the new Charter at the Court House:

> I have myself the happiness of being relieved from the Criminal and Appeal Judicial Duties which were assigned to me by the previous Charter; and you, Gentlemen, cannot but look upon it as an additional mark of his Majesty's confidence in your justice and integrity, that the Civil Jurisdiction of the Assessors in the Supreme Court is now extended without Appeal, as high as £300 sterling; and the only Appeal now, for matters of a higher value, is to his Majesty himself.

This Charter marks a decisive point in the transition of Gibraltar from a garrison to a colony, but it is not quite clear when the change of status became official.

The Police and the Debtors' Prison

The foundation of Gibraltar's police force (now the Royal Gibraltar Police) is often dated to the same time, 1830, just after the establishment of a police force in Britain, when it was formally established under civilian direction; but the police force developed by General Don on his arrival in Gibraltar in 1814, although its primary rôle was to supervise health and hygiene, was also concerned with public order, and can claim to be the true precursor of the present force. The town was divided into districts, each with a sergeant, under the Town Major, who was a military man.

Sergeant Anton,[9] referring to the period before 1830, confirms that the main aim of Don's police force was to maintain public order, and remarks that crime was unusual.

> The police of Gibraltar is well conducted, and crime is a rare occurrence. In the course of six years and upward that the regiment was stationed here [1825-1832], only one execution

86

took place, and that was of the execrable Benito de Sota [sic], a Portuguese pirate, who fled hither from Cadiz, where his wicked crew had been apprehended and executed; and here he met with the fate he so richly deserved.

The debtors' prison, which was in a building near to the Moorish Castle, which was then as now the civil prison, but also had a military section, was another area where Don exerted his beneficence.

The debtors' prison of Gibraltar was at one time a disgrace to humanity. It is situated near the Moorish Castle, and was crowded, ill ventilated, and without any ground for the purposes of exercise, or any screen to protect the unfortunate inmates from the public gaze. Derangement of intellect is mentioned by Mr Frazer [the Principal Medical Officer] as a frequent occurrence in this wretched place. Sir George Don has ameliorated this institution: an enclosed yard has been annexed to the prison, into which the cells open; these cells are about nine feet square, and are perforated by a loophole on the side opposite the door, for the purposes of ventilation. [10]

The Grand Jury's report of January 1815 had pointed out the deplorable state of the Debtors' prison, and also recommended improvements to the jail, or its transfer to a purpose-built building. But nearly two centuries later, the jail is still in the Moorish Castle. They also recommended a 'House of Correction,' where young and less hardened criminals could be rehabilitated, but as far as can be seen nothing was done about this forward-looking proposal.

Education: The Garrison Schools.

Before Don's arrival in Gibraltar, there was little organised education in Gibraltar. There were regimental schools, which had been established on the orders of the Duke of Kent, and the civilians had the benefit only of private academies of variable quality and permanence.

George Don established two Garrison Schools, to coordinate the education of the children of the soldiers. The North Garrison School was situated in Castle Road, just behind the Civil Hospital. The building is still in existence, and was in use as a school until very recently. The South Garrison School was situated on Naval Hospital Hill, just below the present Royal Naval Hospital. The system to be used was that of Andrew Bell, who was one of the founders of a Society for universal elementary education which in 1814 had been renamed 'The British and Foreign School Society'.[11]

Although the schools were set up primarily for the education of Services children, there were also adult education classes (82 privates and NCOs were enrolled in the North Garrison School alone), and civilian children could attend the school on payment of an entry fee of one dollar, and one dollar a month. Children of poor parents were sometimes admitted free at the request of the Lieutenant Governor. It seems that Maria Don was a partner in this project of her husband's; the minutes of the Gibraltar Garrison Library for the 31st March 1815 record that 100 copies of 'Bell's System' had been ordered on behalf of Mrs Don, and in 1818, 'in the presence of His Excellency the Lieutenant Governor', she was one of the examiners of the needlework of the girls in the Garrison Schools. Don then presented prizes 'silver spoons, prayer books etc' to the pupils who showed 'proficiency and regularity'.[12]

This innovation in education in Gibraltar lasted only a few years. In 1828, the Barrack Master found himself in need of accommodation for the troops, and the schools were closed down and used as barracks:

The increase in the number of notices in the *Gibraltar Chronicle* in the years following the closure, advertising the opening of private schools both for boys and for girls, is a measure of the interest in the education of children which had been awakened by the Dons. Dr Hennen questioned the quality of these private tutors and schools:[13]

> There is no respectable seminary of education for children of the better classes. Each regiment has its school for the children of the soldiers; and there are a few day-schools kept by Spanish, Italian, and English residents on a very small scale. Many of the latter are kept in crowded rooms, but as the hours of study are few, it is probable that no bad consequences of a general character have resulted from them.

88

It would appear that the ill-effects which Hennen was worried about were from the overcrowding, rather than poor teaching.

In August 1828, Don was still hoping that the schools would soon be reopened, but it was only in September 1832, a few months after his death, that the Gibraltar Public School was opened by Don's successor, Sir William Houstoun, using the money left over from the account of the Garrison Schools, which Don had carefully salted away in 1828.

Religious Denominations and the Garrison Church

After the capture of Gibraltar in 1704, most of the Roman Catholic convents and places of worship were closed down. Only 'the Spanish Church' in Main Street (now the Cathedral of St. Mary the Crowned) remained for the Catholic inhabitants, while the chapel attached to the Franciscan Convent was taken over by the garrison and became the only Anglican place of worship. This was completely inadequate for the Protestant population, and was able to accommodate only the officers and a few well -to- do British inhabitants. The rank and file attended divine service on the parade grounds, in all weathers.

Shortly after his arrival,[14] Don was made aware of this lack, and he proposed that the old White Cloister could be converted as a Protestant church, but nothing was done until 1819 [15], when a James Arberry petitioned the Treasury for a Protestant church for Gibraltar, and Don, asked to comment, was 'of the opinion that such an establishment would be highly desirable'. A meeting of Protestant inhabitants was held in Gibraltar, and subscriptions were solicited for the building of a church. Don promised $500, and selected a site on Governor's Parade for the new church. The Treasury gave permission for £5000 to be used - but it had to come out of Gibraltar revenues. Don's multiple projects meant that money was short at the time, and the idea was temporarily dropped.

Lord Chatham, when he took over command of the Rock in 1821 and Don went into temporary retirement in San Roque, reopened the subject, suggesting that the White Cloister could be sold and the church built with the money raised. A plainer church, he thought, could be built with the sum that the White Cloister would fetch - the original plan for the church which Don had had drawn up had been quite elaborate. Col. Pilkington, Commander of the Royal Engineers, drew up plans; the style was to be Moorish, in memory of the long Moorish occupation of Gibraltar, and there were to be separate entrances for civilians and the military. Chatham laid the foundation stone, and left Gibraltar a few days later, and Don was again in charge.

The next few years saw delay after delay. Bad weather delayed the building, there were disputes with the builder, Adam Moir, money was short; on one occasion the plans were lost. Then came the yellow fever epidemic of 1828, and the shell of the church was used as Auxiliary Hospital No 1. Both Colonel Pilkington and Don were censured by Whitehall at one time or another for the delays.

Sgt. Anton[16] was of the opinion that Don did not show much enthusiasm about the building of the church:

> A church had been lately built in the town, but owing to the indifference of the Lieutenant Governor, Sir George Don, it was permitted to remain for several years in an unfinished state. A large sum had been expended on its erection, and it was likely to fall to decay before it was completed, although very much wanted...

But on January 4th 1832, General Sir George Don was buried in the new church where a monument still stands to his memory. The church was indeed not completed until September 1832, and only consecrated as the Garrison Church in 1836, in the presence of Queen Adelaide, the wife of William IV. Later, it became the Cathedral of the Holy Trinity.

Don extended his consideration to other religions within the community. He was initially suspicious of the Catholic community, and especially of the priesthood, whom he feared might favour Spain over Britain, and might even subvert the Irish regiments under his command (see Appendix II). On one occasion at least, two Jesuit missionaries from Spain were deported as suspicious characters. Irish soldiers were not even allowed to attend services in the local

Catholic church until the passing of the Catholic Emanciparion Act in Britain in 1829.

Don had a clash with the Vicar Apostolic, Father Isidro Dominguez, over his plan for a new hospital, which would supersede the little remnant of the *Hospital de San Juan de Dios,* which the Catholic community kept behind the Spanish Church. Father Dominguez resigned, perhaps because of this: Caruana[17] describes General Don's angry reaction to Father Dominguez's objections; but Dominguez was also under pressure from the Catholic Junta of Elders, who had accused him of fraud and of neglecting his religious duties.[18] He was cleared of this accusation by the Vatican, but was replaced by Father Juan Bautista Zino, who seems to have got on rather better with the Junta, and with Don, who gave him permission to open a church in the North Front for the use of Catholics residing in the summer village.

When the Civil Hospital was built, it was, as we have seen, divided into three sections, one for each of the three main religious groups, the Catholics, Protestants and Jews, who each managed the affairs of their section with almost complete independence.

His relations with the Jews - he always referred to the Jewish community as 'The Hebrew Nation' - seems to have been at least cordial. He consulted their representatives on matters that concerned them, and was on good terms with the leaders of the community, such as Judah Benoliel and Aaron Cardozo, although he fell out with Cardozo over the Titles to Lands issue.

In his relations with the Methodists he demonstrated a sense of fairness that former governors had often not shown. When the Military Chaplains refused to allow Methodist Ministers to baptise, and refused to bury anyone baptised by them, the matter was brought to Don, who sought a legal opinion, and was happy to abide by the decision that Methodist baptisms were legal.

In 1818, after an Anglican clergyman had refused to bury a child on the grounds that he had not baptised it, the Methodists appealed to Don, and asked for a section of the cemetery to be allocated to them. Official sanction was given for a Methodist cemetery but because of opposition from the main Christian

91

denominations, the Methodists were allocated a piece of ground outside the main cemetery and some distance from it. Don was petitioned, and went himself to inspect the plot. The result was that the Methodists were given a plot within the main cemetery. He also renewed the lease of the Methodist Chapel – the Providence Chapel – at a nominal rent. Don also ruled that sick servicemen in hospital could be seen by the minister of their choice, including the Methodists; in addition, he sanctioned that the ration allocated to civil officers be extended to the Methodist minister, thus accepting his official standing in the establishment.[19]

The Methodists received bibles from the British and Foreign Bible Society for distribution in Gibraltar, and they also wished to distribute them in Spain as well. Don did not approve of this, as he felt that it would imperil Gibraltar's good relations with Catholic Spain;[20] as George Borrow was to discover only a few years later, the Spanish authorities did not take kindly to the distribution of Protestant Bibles within their territory.[21]

During the disastrous yellow fever epidemic of 1828, when the Church of England chaplain died of the fever, the Methodist Minister, William Barber, conducted the Protestant funerals, presumably with the Lieutenant Governor's acquiescence, until he himself died a few days later, when an army lieutenant was deputed to carry out this duty.[22]

The Gibraltar Garrison Library [23]

The Garrison Library was founded in 1793, and transferred to its present building which was built for the purpose, in 1804, so it was already a well-established institution by the time that Don arrived. He was elected President of the Library on his arrival, and attended meetings of the Committee regularly in the early years. Don remained President of the Library even when Chatham was in residence in Gibraltar (1821-25). Chatham was named Patron during this period, but took little interest in the Library (and not much in anything else).

George Don always maintained his involvement with the Library, and presented it with books and maps. He also used the Library to order books for himself and for his projects for the betterment of Gibraltar.

He obtained the portrait of Colonel Drinkwater, which hangs in the upper Reading Room, and was responsible for a new Constitution for the Library in 1817.

On one occasion, the committee fined Sir George Don one dollar for bringing his dog into the library. Don himself presided at that meeting!

Other buildings

Casemates Barracks were completed in 1817 by Don (the adjacent Casemates Gate bears the name of the Governor, the Earl of Chatham).

An Officer's Hospital was built on Europa Flats in 1817. This became a barracks in 1826, and is now known as Bleak House. Don also rebuilt and extended Governor's Cottage, where he spent much of his time, especially during the years when Chatham was in residence at the Convent.

At the back of the Rock, to the eastward, is the Governor's summer residence, offering, however, nothing remarkable in its construction or situation, being a low, ill-built, half-stone, half-wooden building. On Europa Flats, Sir George Don has erected a very handsome hospital, of lofty, cool, and capacious wards, intended as a reserve against the breaking out of any dangerous fever; where the sick may be nursed without the least fear of infecting the other parts of the rock; but thanks to his watchfulness and good arrangements, he has made his foresight unavailable, as it has never yet been used for the intended purpose. The situation of this building is one of the most appropriate, in my opinion, for the Governor's summer residence. Its exposure to the eastern and western breezes, renders it the coolest situation of the two...[24]

Beauclerk's optimism about the health of Gibraltar was soon to be shattered.

NOTES

1. Calderón Quijano.
2. Hennen, p. 72.
3. Ibid. p. 71.

4. Sweetland, W. *Observations on the Trade of Gibraltar*. Manuscript included in Governors' Letters, GGA. Sweetland was Captain of the Port, and wrote a lengthy but interesting account of the trading fortunes of Gibraltar from 1793 to 1829, for Sir George Don, who had received a request for this from Sir George Murray, the Secretary of State for the Colonies.

5. *Gibraltar Chronicle*, 29th August 1818.

6. James Bell; Ford, Vol. II, p 613 of the 1966 reprint.

7. Benady, T, p. xiii.

8. Don to Bathurst. Governors' Letters 4th August 1816. GGA.

9. Anton J, p. 362.

10. Don to Bathurst. Governors' Letters 14th April 1817. GGA; Hennen. op. cit., p. 86; CO 91/63, 03672.

11. Traverso. Much of the material in this section is from pp. 1-15.

12. *Gibraltar Chronicle*, 4th April 1818.

13. Hennen, p. 81.

14. Don to Bathurst. Governors letters, 10th Jan. 1815. GGA; Simpson. The rest of this section is taken largely from this work.

15. Anton, p. 341.

16. Caruana, pp. 41-42, 47.

17. Public Records Office. CO 91/66.

18. Anon (2), pp. 17-18, 20.

19. Mrs Nicklin to the British and Foreign Bible Society, 3 May 1819. Mrs Caroline Nicklin was a Methodist shop owner in Gibraltar who sold or distributed Bibles free in her establishment. She is the only woman whose name appears on the plaque recording the founders of the Exchange in the foyer of the present House of Assembly.

20. Borrow, G.

21. *Ibid* p. 18.

22. Gibraltar Garrison Library Minutes, *passim*.

23. Beauclerk.

Chapter 9

DEFENCE AND EXTERNAL AFFAIRS

Defence

As the military commander of the Garrison of Gibraltar, George Don was of course responsible for the security of the Rock. The main potential threat, as ever, was Spain. Even though Britain and Spain had been allies against Napoleon, Don recognised that Spain's attitude to a British Gibraltar had not changed and would not change: 'I positively know that even at this moment when the country is sunk so low the feelings of the Spaniards with respect to Gibraltar remain steadily the same,' he wrote in 1816.[1]

Certainly the threat from France had disappeared since Napoleon had left the scene, although there must have been renewed anxiety in the early days after Don's arrival in Gibraltar - the '100 days' between Buonaparte's escape from Elba and the Battle of Waterloo. But after Waterloo, there was no need in Gibraltar for the intense and urgent activity with which Don had fortified Jersey against attack. Roads were indeed built, as they had been in Jersey, but they were built to make life easier for the Royal Calpe Hunt, to improve communications with San Roque, where Don spent much of his time and, perhaps not entirely incidentally, for the benefit of the inhabitants of the area.

Relations across the frontier with Spain must have been strained at one point, when in 1814 the newly reinstated King Fernando VII ordered the reconstruction of the Spanish Lines - the defensive wall across the isthmus from the Bay to the Mediterranean, which Spain had built after the siege of 1727, and which had been dismantled by the Royal Engineers, on the orders of the Lieutenant Governor, General Colin Campbell, in 1810.

When he heard of the plan to rebuilt the Lines, Don's message to General Alós was sharp and unceremonious:

Stop the works immediately. If you start them again, I will fire a gun. If that is not enough, I will fire another. If you continue, I will fire a broadside! [2]

Or so the Spanish author reports; but the same author also laments the destruction of the Lines in 1810, calling it 'cruel', ignoring the fact that the demolition had been ordered only after General Campbell, the Lieutenant Governor who preceded Don, had sought and received approval from the Spanish Junta in Seville, in order to prevent the advancing French Army from using the fortifications in a possible assault on the Rock.

By 1816, with Napoleon now safely out of the way in captivity in St. Helena, Whitehall decided that it was time to reduce the military expenditure in Gibraltar. Don's reply, reproduced in full in Appendix II, argues strongly for improving the defences, in particular in the North Front, and complains that the building of Casemates Barracks has been delayed because of previous budgetary cuts. His protests must have had some effect, because the Barracks were completed in the following year, although works in the area continued for some years, as the new Casemates Gate bears the name of the Earl of Chatham, who did not come to Gibraltar until 1821.

At the same time Don noted another deficiency in the security of Gibraltar – 'the lack of a citadel.' Obviously, he was thinking back to Jersey, where he had seen the completion of the great citadel of Fort Regent which dominates St. Helier. He felt that in Gibraltar, a citadel was essential not just as a bulwark against attack from the outside (the old Moorish Castle had long outlived its usefulness as a defensive asset), but as a means of controlling possible civil unrest. This last consideration had not been a serious issue in Jersey, where the population was well-established, and had regarded itself as British for centuries, but in Gibraltar he found himself with a largely Roman Catholic population, including many recent immigrants, which he feared might side with Spain in the event of war; indeed, he was even suspicious of the Catholic officers and men of the regiments defending the Garrison, whom he thought might be influenced to rebel by their co-religionaries within the civilian population and in Spain.

Don expressed another concern in his letter to Lord Bathurst. He felt that the soldiers of the Garrison had to perform guard duty too often, and did not get enough rest. He used this argument to support his plea for a larger garrison, but he must also have been motivated by a genuine concern for the well-being of his men. Certainly, his efforts to improve the health of the garrison and population of Gibraltar, although partly motivated, no doubt, by a desire to keep the force defending Gibraltar as effective as possible, demonstrate the depth of his humanitarian feelings.

George Don's review in 1816 of the state of the defences of Gibraltar must have been considered authoritative by Whitehall, as no further review was called for until 1834, over two years after Don's death.[3]

Spain

Geographical and historical reality dictates that Gibraltar's most important neighbour is Spain, the country which lies on the other side of Gibraltar's only land frontier, and the country which had lost Gibraltar in 1704, during the War of the Spanish Succession, and had failed to get it back in spite of three bloody sieges in the eighteenth century. In part because of Britain's continued possession of Gibraltar, the two countries had been enemies almost continuously for over a century. However, by the time that George Don arrived in Gibraltar, Britain and Spain had been allies for six years, ever since the Spaniards had rebelled against King Joseph, Napoleon Bonaparte's brother, known derisively to them as 'Pepe Botella', and had combined with the British forces under the Duke of Wellington to drive the French army out of Spain in the Peninsular War (1808-1814).

Don's only experience of the Spaniards as soldiers had been during the siege of Fort St. Philip, in Minorca, in 1782, at the same time that Gibraltar was suffering its last and most severe siege, the Great Siege of 1779-83. On that occasion, Gibraltar had survived, but Minorca fell to a largely Spanish force, in spite of the tenacious defence led by General Murray, Maria Don's uncle; George Don

97

would have had a healthy respect for the Spaniard as a fighting man.

But now Britain and Spain were at peace, and were allies. As soon as General Don arrived in Gibraltar, he began to make contact with his counterpart on the other side of the frontier, Lieutenant General José María Alós, the Commandant of the *Campo de Gibraltar*, who was based in Algeciras, across the Bay. In December 1814, when he had barely set foot on dry land, Don wrote that he was arranging to extend a road which the Spaniards were building from San Roque as far as the British Lines, and that he was looking forward to meeting Alós in the near future.

There may have been misunderstandings at first - one author [4] remarked that Don's name always puzzled the Spaniards, who would ask ``Don who?''

Whatever unpleasantness which could have been occasioned by the episode recounted above, when Don peremptorily forbade the rebuilding of the Spanish Defences, does not seem to have soured relations for long, or to have inhibited the spirit of co-operation between the two generals; and in 1817 this spirit was put to the test.

The bubonic plague had appeared in Morocco, and was killing its thousands on the African side of the Straits; it was essential to prevent it crossing the water, and Don wrote to Lord Bathurst: 'The Spanish General commanding in the adjoining District has taken the necessary precautions to prevent the introduction of the Plague into this part of Spain and we heartily co-operate together in the execution of the measures, which have been proposed.' [5]

The energetic measures taken by Don and Alós in concert have been described in Chapter 6, and there can be little doubt that the vigilance of Don and Alós saved Europe from another disastrous epidemic which could have been as disastrous as the Black Death. A few cases were seen in Mallorca, but mainland Europe remained free of the disease. Don's close relationship with General Alós throughout this crisis may also have helped later, when Alós became Fernando VII's Minister for War.

In 1820, yellow fever reappeared in Southern Spain, and Don ordered the closure of the frontier by a cordon, although markets

98

were allowed on the Neutral Ground, with arrangements for the transfer of goods and money that were probably similar to those described by Anton [6] in 1828 when Gibraltar had been attacked by yellow fever and the rôles were reversed. During this latter epidemic, Spain demonstrated her generosity to Gibraltar, when the King ordered that 20,000 fanegas of flour be sent to Gibraltar to relieve the population there, which was in danger of going hungry.[7]

There were moments of conflict. In 1825, two British ships went aground in the Neutral Ground, and were impounded by Spain.[8] The Gibraltar merchants appealed to Don, who sent the Navy to secure the release of the ships, and Madrid protested angrily to the British Government, but to no avail.

In general, however, Don seems to have managed to keep on good terms with Alós and his successors. As so often in the history of Gibraltar, relations with the hinterland remained good, although the central government of Spain might fire off protests to Britain from time to time.

George Don's good relations with the authorities in the Campo de Gibraltar were without doubt helped by his evident love for the area. He lost no time after arriving in buying a house in San Roque, in San Felipe Street, and later was granted an adjoining piece of land, presumably to build an extension.[9]

He spent as much of his time there as his duties allowed. Montero, who was himself a native of San Roque, wrote in his *Historia de Gibraltar*: [10]

> His memory is also cherished in the towns of the Campo, especially in San Roque, where he would spend the greater part of each year. He was fond of the Spaniards, and he was happy to live among them, and he would travel through the countryside and farms spreading largesse.

Montero was writing at a time when Don and his achievements were within living memory; even after thirty years, this memory was fresh in the Campo.

One of his officers, Captain Rochfort Scott, describes an incident in San Roque, which illustrates Sir George Don's kindly nature; on this occasion it nearly came into conflict with his need to demonstrate diplomatic correctness while he was a guest in Spain, at a time when there was a certain amount of tension because of Don's tacit protection of Spanish Liberals who had sought and obtained asylum on the Rock from the repressive regime of Fernando VII.[11]

> I was seated one morning tête-à-tête with the General... when we observed a guard of Spanish soldiers pass by the window, headed by an officer on horseback, and having a prisoner in charge; and to our astonishment they stopped at the General's door....
>
> The prisoner rushed in, announced that he was Prince Lucien Murat (the son of General Murat, who had been appointed King of Naples by Napoleon) and that he had been lured into Spain from Gibraltar, and was now being taken to Algeciras, where he would undoubtedly be murdered. He now wished to put himself under British protection.
>
> 'Monsieur,' replied the General, with no slight astonishment, 'this is indeed a very extraordinary, and apparently most unjustifiable proceeding; but I am sorry to inform you that I can afford you no *protection*. The British flag does not fly at San Roque; and I myself reside here only by permission of the Spanish Government. My good offices, - as far as they can be of service in liberating you, - shall not be wanting....'

Murat had previously been expelled from Spain to Gibraltar, with a warning that he would be arrested if he attempted to return, but the General wrote to General O'Donnell, commander of the Spanish forces in the *Campo de Gibraltar*, in Algeciras, requesting that the ex-Prince should be treated with respect and attention. Since O'Donnell owed the Lieutenant Governor a favour – Don had given asylum to O'Donnell's wife and children in Gibraltar when the Liberals were in power (see below) - he heeded Don's request. Lucien Murat survived, although he was jailed in Algeciras until he could be put on the first available vessel to the United States.

The Spanish Liberals in Gibraltar

During the Peninsular War, while Fernando VII was in exile, the Spanish Liberals had formed a Government in Cadiz and proclaimed the Constitution of 1812. When Fernando returned to Spain in 1814,

100

he at first promised to uphold the Constitution, but then almost immediately repudiated it and tried to rule as an absolute monarch. This led many Spanish Liberals to flee from his persecution, and some of these found refuge in Gibraltar.

By 1819, the Spanish American Colonies were in revolt, and Fernando ordered an army to be assembled in lower Andalusia, which was to sail to South America to fight the rebellious colonists.[12] This army became the nucleus of an insurrection which forced Fernando to promise to restore the 1812 Constitution, although General O'Donnell, who was a monarchist at the time, was able to contain the revolt in Andalusia at first. Don's first involvement was to grant asylum to O'Donnell's wife and two children, who had to flee from Algeciras to Gibraltar.[13] Even at this time, the Spanish Government was complaining that Gibraltar had become a refuge for Liberal dissidents. Most of these returned to Spain while the Liberals were in temporary power during the *Trienio Liberal* (1820-1823).

These Liberal Constitutionalists formed the Spanish Government until 1823, when France sent an army into Spain to restore Fernando's absolute power. The French army quickly overran Spain, and attacked Cadiz, where the Liberals had taken the King. The Liberals had to surrender Fernando in October 1823, and that unamiable monarch, after promising an amnesty, changed his mind the next day, and ordered the arrest of all Liberal sympathisers. Those Liberals who were able to escape fled the country, many of them to Gibraltar, where they were given asylum. Many of the Spanish Liberals used Gibraltar as a staging post on their way to exile in Britain or South America, but others remained. One of the refugees was an English volunteer, Robert Wilson, who was much later to become Governor of Gibraltar (1842-1848). Thomas Steele,[14] who was himself one of their number, states that at the time the streets of Gibraltar were crowded with Liberal refugees.

Most of the inhabitants, including some of the more influential ones, were in sympathy with the refugees, and took many of them into their homes: [15]

101

At the mansion of the princely Cardozo, on the sea side of the square, one might observe some distinguished Spaniard inquiring after the health of his guest, General Quiroga, who was feverish and confined to his bed... I found Cardozo sitting by the bedside of his distinguished guest and performing the gentler rites of hospitality and kindness...

Aaron Cardozo was one of the most influential members of the Jewish community of Gibraltar; he had been an important supplier to the Navy during the Napoleonic Wars, and had become a close friend of Nelson. In fact he had twenty refugees as house guests at the time, including Sir Robert Wilson. His mansion is now the City Hall.

The British Government, in the person of the Governor, Lord Chatham (Don was at the time in temporary retirement in his house in San Roque) were embarrassed by the refugees, whose presence in the garrison was sure to offend both Spain and France, and attempted to move them on as quickly as they could. The British volunteers could stay, of course, but the Spaniards must go. He gave one of their leaders, General Alava, an ultimatum: the Spanish Liberals must leave on a given date. He added that Alava himself could stay as his guest, and got a predictably haughty reply: 'No, my Lord. I am also a Spanish refugee, and as my companions are ordered out of the town, I will go too.'[16] Most of the Spaniards left, but some remained, either concealed by Gibraltarian sympathizers in the town, or in the hulks moored in the Bay.

In August 1824 some of the refugees in Gibraltar attempted an invasion, led by Colonel Francisco Valdés. The insurgents had some initial successes, and succeeded in capturing Tarifa, but were rapidly and brutally crushed by O'Donnell. Thirty-six of the most prominent Liberals were shot out of hand, and the rest (100) were put on trial, and many of these were also executed. When Colonel Valdés. who had survived, attempted to re-enter Gibraltar in 1825, he was refused admittance, but was given passage to England.

The Liberal refugees who remained in Gibraltar during the latter half of the 1820s, when Don was again in command, seem to have been tacitly tolerated there, in spite of launching repeated but

102

ineffective attacks on the coasts of Spain. In one such attack, they actually drove the small Spanish garrison from La Linea to Campamento, where it had to be reinforced; and when the Spanish troops counter-attacked, the insurgents themselves had to take to their heels and beg for asylum at the Gibraltar frontier gates.

Other Liberals used Gibraltar as a base for attacks on Spanish ships, using vessels flying the Colombian flag, and on one occasion at least, took the crew of a Spanish ship prisoners of war.[17] They sold their booty with impunity in the Bay.

> The lieutenant governor was far from countenancing this lawless measure; but as no insult was offered to the British flag, nor any breach of peace committed within the bound of his government, he had no cause to interfere.[18]

One of the most prominent of the Liberal refugees was General Torrijos, who had been Minister for War in the Liberal administration. Having failed in an attempt to raise an insurrection in Cadiz, he fled to Gibraltar, where he formed a Government-in-exile. His presence on the Rock caused Madrid to threaten restrictions at the frontier, and in an attempt to avert this, Don arranged for him to be sent to Malta aboard a Royal Navy frigate, and wrote personally to Fernado VII to confirm that this had been carried out. Communications with Spain were restored, and the departure of the frigate *Actaeon* was reported in Spain with delight. But the man on board was not Torrijos, but a look-alike, and the rebel general remained in Gibraltar, concealed by his friends among the civil population.[19] It is difficult to believe that Don could have known nothing of this deception.

Later, Torrijos led an incursion near Algeciras in January 1831, which also failed, and he had to re-embark hastily for Gibraltar. His end came in December 1831, when he was betrayed by an old friend, the Military Governor of Malaga, who sent messages to Torrijos through agents, leading him to believe that he would join him in a revolt. Torrijos landed in Malaga with 200 men, and was promptly arrested and shot together with all his companions, including a young Irish volunteer, Lieutenant Robert Boyd, who had financed the expedition.

103

Don seems to have been as sympathetic to the Liberal refugees as far as his duty of maintaining good relations with Spain allowed. Montero [20] remarks that the Governors of Gibraltar had need of a great deal of tact and prudence to prevent the Spanish Government regarding the asylum afforded to the emigrants as an act of hostility; and that this danger was avoided by the fine judgement of General Don, who had returned to command the Garrison on the departure in 1825 of Lord Chatham, thus avoiding that the matter should give rise to any disagreeable complication between the two governments.

Morocco

It was just as important to maintain good relations with the Empire of Morocco, which was even more unstable than Spain. Much of Gibraltar's supplies was imported from across the Straits, and the Garrison would be even more dependent on this source of food, as it had been throughout most of the eighteenth century, should there ever be another rift with Spain.

Don's task was easier there than with Spain. Cordial relations were easily established by the exchange of flowery letters of compliments between himself (in the name of King George III) and the Emperor. The demands made by the Emperor and his minions in Tangier were also easily to meet.

At the request of the Emperor, Don sent medical officers to treat Moroccan notables,[21] who had a high opinion of British medicine. This practice was of long standing, an early Army medical officer who was sent to Morocco to treat a son of the then Emperor being Dr William Lempriere,[22] who wrote an account of his experiences in 1793.

The Emperor made frequent requests for 'presents' mainly of artillery, and was easily satisfied by the despatch of mainly obsolete cannon. On occasion, a request would be made for passage on a British man-of-war for one of the Emperor's relatives, and this type of request was also easy to comply with.

There was a temporary crisis late in 1828, when Don ordered Tangier to be blockaded, apparently because of difficulties made by the Moroccan authorities in supplying Gibraltar during the yellow

104

fever epidemic, but this does not seem to have caused any permanent souring of relations.

Piracy

The privateering activities of the liberal refugees against Spanish ships was not the only form of piracy which was practiced in the Straits of Gibraltar at the time, and Sir George Don dealt severely with anyone whom he caught within his jurisdiction.

The most notorious pirate to be tried in Gibraltar was Benito de Soto. In a career lasting barely six months, between Rio de Janeiro and Cadiz, he and his crew boarded and plundered six ships, setting them on fire, and murdering many seamen. When he finally ran his ship *El Defensor de Pedro* on to the shore at Cadiz, he and his crew were arrested. Ten of the crew were executed, but de Soto escaped to what he hoped was the safe refuge of Gibraltar. He was to be disappointed; he was again arrested. He was found guilty of piracy by the Admiralty session after a trial lasting ten hours, and sentenced by General Sir George Don to death by hanging. He was duly hanged on a gallows specially set up on the Glacis, just outside the walls of the town, on January 25th, 1830.

According to the *Gibraltar Directory and Guidebook*, when he was led before the gallows

> He harangued the surrounding populace in Spanish, acknowledging the justice of his sentence and exhorting them to take warning of his death and asking for their prayers. He found the halter too high and he boldly stepped upon his coffin and placed his neck to the noose, passing into eternity without the slightest struggle.[23]

The Slave Trade

Gibraltar, in common with many of the ports bordering on the Atlantic, had long been used by slave traders as a base for outfitting their ships before embarking on slaving trips. When Britain decreed that the slave trade was to be abolished, this practice, long profitable to the merchants of Gibraltar, could obviously no longer be tolerated.

A proclamation by Don on July 8th 1829 stated that certain vessels had resorted to the Bay to be equipped for the slave trade, and that henceforth the Secretary of State for the Colonies prohibited any ship from receiving in Gibraltar any assistance in furtherance of the slave trade.

With the help of the British Consuls in Spanish ports, especially Consul Archdeakin in Cadiz, Don and his Captain of the Port, William Sweetland, were kept informed of any suspicious ships that were heading towards Gibraltar, and such vessels were rigorously inspected for any sign that they planned to engage in the slave trade.

Ironically, it was the civil population, whose rights Sir George Don had done so much to foster, who banded together to oppose their Lieutenant Governor, fearing that business would be lost as a result of his prohibition of commerce with the slave traders, but to no avail. Don, as usual, had his way.[24]

NOTES

1. Don to Bathurst. Governors Letters 20th July 1816. GGA. This letter, the full text of which is given in Appendix II, is the source for much of the material in this section.
2. Luna, p. 62.
3. *Report on the Colonial Military Expenditure.* House of Commons, 1834. p 5.
4. Ticknor. Vol. I. p 235n.
5. Don to Bathurst, 22 June 1818. Governors Letters, GGA.
6. Anton, pp. 348-350.
7. Don. Governors Letters, 20th Oct. 1828. GGA.
8. Hills, p. 375.
9. Caldelas Lopez, p. 112.
10. Montero, p. 403.
11. Scott, Vol. I, pp. 44-51.
12. Don to Bathurst, 20th June 1820. Governors Letters, GGA.
13. Don to Bathurst, 20th February 1820. Governors Letters, GGA.
14. Steele, p. 214.
15. Ibid. p. 215.
16. Ibid. p. 239
17. Don. Governors Letters, 29th December 1825, 27th April 1826, 4th December 1826.
18. Anton, p. 362.
19. Plá, pp. 106-107.
20. Montero, p. 404.

21. Beauclerk, passim.
22. Lempriere, W.
23. *Gibraltar Directory and Guidebook for 1930.*
24. Sepúlveda, p. 187.

Chapter 10

YELLOW FEVER STRIKES AGAIN

Nearly fourteen years had passed since George Don arrived in Gibraltar and was faced by an epidemic of yellow fever – the 1814 epidemic, the fourth in a decade – and as he approached the end of a long career, he might have been justified in hoping that the measures he had taken to make Gibraltar a healthier place had borne fruit, and that the city would be spared another major epidemic.

In 1826, Captain Beauclerk[1] had written

...the town has become a remarkably neat, comfortable place of residence, and nothing can exceed the high state of health of the people. Since the arrival of Sir George Don, the Lieutenant Governor of the place, it has not been visited by any sickness.

But this happy state of affairs was not to last much longer. On September 1, 1828, a washerwoman died of yellow fever in the 24th District, and within a few days, other cases were diagnosed, at first in the same vicinity, and then outside it, throughout the Garrison. Civilians and soldiers alike were dying in droves.

It seems as if at first Don did not want to believe that it could be happening: his letters to Earl Bathurst play down the gravity of the situation;[2] he asked four doctors to visit the district where the fever had occurred, the hospitals and the church (this last presumably to question the priest about deaths due to fever) and when they reported that 'the Garrison has not been so healthy these last ten years,' he was happy to accept their judgement.

The Spanish authorities were less sanguine. A Spanish medical commission visited Gibraltar from Algeciras on September 4th, and recommended the establishment of a sanitary cordon at the border. General Miranda, the officer then commanding at Algeciras, immediately sent 200 troops to set up a sanitary cordon at the frontier, and later enforced a cordon around the whole Campo area, but it was probably due to Don's good relations with the Spanish authorities that an embargo on the importation of essential foods was never enforced, and customs duties on foodstuffs were even waived.

Complicated arrangements were put in place at the frontier in an attempt to prevent the transfer of infection. The Spanish established a cordon on their side of the border, and the Gibraltar authorities set up their own cordon at a distance of fifty paces. The Spanish merchants then brought their articles to the centre of the space between the cordons, and withdrew. The Gibraltarian buyers would then negotiate a price with the Spaniards by shouting from cordon to cordon, and then advance, collect their bargains, and leave payment, which was placed in pails of vinegar to 'sterilize' it and only then collected by the sellers.[3]

Later, the King of Spain, Fernando VII, was to send a donation of 10,000 *fanegas* (about 600,000 lb) of wheat to supply the poor of Gibraltar, with the promise of another 10,000 *fanegas* should they be required. He also suspended the duties on food imported across the frontier.

When Dr John Hennen, the Principal Medical Officer of the Garrison, asked Don a few days later to form a Board of Health to deal with the problem, as had been done in the past, Don refused, saying that all measures recommended by the Boards of Health in earlier epidemics had already been put into place.[4]

As the number of cases and the deaths increased, Don was forced to recognise the gravity of the situation, but he remained optimistic, at least in his despatches to Whitehall, in which he looked forward to the disease ending with the coming of the rains and cooler weather, as it had done in the past.

The measures which he had taken seem to have had some effect; he moved as many of the troops as he could out of the crowded town area, and provided tents for a camp in the Neutral Ground for several thousand indigent civilians from the most crowded areas of the town, in addition to the village of huts in the same area where many of the inhabitants regularly spent the summer as a precautionary measure. Later on in the epidemic, Don ordered several large wooden buildings to be erected to accommodate people convalescing from the fever, thus freeing hospital beds for the acutely sick.

His private arrangements followed the same rule. He removed his whole establishment, a total of 56 people, to Governor's Cottage in Europa, and allowed none of them to go to the town apart from himself and an attendant, with whom he rode into town every day to carry out his duties.[5] Apart from one of the attendants who had accompanied him, who suffered a mild attack of fever, Don and his establishment escaped infection, as did nearly all of those soldiers and civilians who he had removed from the town area.

By mid-October there had been five hundred deaths, and the epidemic still showed no sign of abating. At Dr Hennen's suggestion, Don ordered the as yet uncompleted Protestant Church to be used as an emergency hospital, as was the Methodist Chapel in Prince Edward's Road, near the site of the first diagnosed cases of yellow fever. When the epidemic was over, the chapel was returned to the Wesleyans, and Don authorised the complete redecoration of the interior at Crown expense in order to make good the damage done during its use as a hospital.[6] An Officers' Hospital was opened in Europa, perhaps in the building now called Bleak House, which was originally built as a hospital, but had hitherto always been used as a barracks.

While the indefatigable and respected physician, John Hennen, was in charge of the medical affairs of the Garrison, the measures which he suggested and which Don put into effect seem to have had the confidence of the people. This was to change. Hennen fell ill with the fever and died. Dr Alexander Broadfoot, who had been Inspector of Quarantine, and whose assistance during his illness Hennen had initially refused, was made Acting Principal Medical Officer by Don. The rumour went round that Don's announcement that Broadfoot was to act as PMO while Hennen was ill had hastened the latter's death, but in fact Hennen had dictated a letter to Don recommending Broadfoot as his assistant just before he died.

110

The Assistant PMO, Dr Dow, wrote indignantly to Don, complaining that he had been passed over, but the Lieutenant Governor justified his action by pointing out that Broadfoot was the senior officer, and so he could not place him under Dow, and he did not wish to fragment the service by putting one of them in charge of the civilian medical service and the other in charge of the Garrison.

The appointment of Broadfoot was popular neither with the public nor the medical profession. He was thought to be a ditherer, issuing orders and then countermanding them. Satirical posters were put up in the town: [7]

> Wanted: for the Public Service, A Principal Medical Officer. He must be a man of sound practical ability. Must possess Common Sense and other requisites to qualify him for the important Trust.
> (N.B. Left handed men not approved of)
> Apply by letter to
> A Bullicugie M.D.
> Insp. of Hospitals *ad interim*.

Perhaps Broadfoot was left-handed. Another was even more abusive:

> Wanted: A skilfull barber to shave the head of the Inspector of Health, apply a cataplasm [a poultice] and administer a clyster [an enema].

Another poster even attacked Don himself, very directly:

> From an Evening Journal, London, 32 Oct
> We understand from good authority that Old Tom Walker has been appointed to supersede the present Lieut. Governor of a certain Rocky Fortress. It is rumoured that the present distribution of places and employment by him or rather by the Cabal that direct him has been the main cause of his removal.
> We approve and rejoice in the adoption of this measure certain as we are that the Public will not be the losers by the exchange of heads.

The controversy was quietened at the end of November, when Don appointed Dr William Pym as Principal Medical Officer in place of Broadfoot. Pym had arrived shortly after Hennen died, sent by the Colonial Secretary to superintend and advise on the management of the epidemic in a civil capacity. Don insisted in appointing him as

PMO – he probably thought it was a good way out of the controversy surrounding Broadfoot and Pym accepted 'after some hesitation from motives of delicacy to Dr. Broadfoot,' he said.[8] Pym was the author of several books on yellow fever, or 'the Bulam Fever', as he called it, and was regarded by many - including himself - as the foremost authority on the disease. He had also served in Gibraltar during the 1804 and 1810 epidemics, and his appointment in place of Broadfoot seems to have been a popular one. On his return to England, he was knighted, and later served as Chairman of the Central Board of Health during the cholera epidemic of 1832 in Britain.

At the same time, three eminent French physicians arrived on the Rock, sent by France to investigate the yellow fever. They were Drs Chervin, Louis and Trousseau, who, together with Dr David Barry, another arrival, formed one of the three committees which sat after the crisis was over to try to elucidate the causes of the yellow fever epidemic.

Barry had also caused some controversy on his arrival, firstly because he challenged Broadfoot's appointment, wishing to be given the job of PMO himself, and later when he convinced one of the Assistant Surgeons to the regiments to stop treating patients with calomel – a wise move, as it happened, but which did not prevent him and the Assistant Surgeon, Dr Galeani, being court-martialled for disobeying orders – and those orders were that calomel was to be given.

In November, Don announced a blockade of the Moroccan port of Tangier, presumably because the authorities there had been making difficulties over supplying the Garrison with food.[9] He was a little nervous about this action, as he feared that the Moroccans might revenge themselves by attacking British merchant vessels. The blockade was lifted in January; by that time, the epidemic was over, and communications with Spain had been reopened

With the onset of cooler weather at the end of the year, the epidemic finally ceased. Colonel Bayly, who had arrived to command the 12th Regiment at the onset of the fever, and who gave a highly coloured account of the epidemic in his memoirs,[10] commented that

112

Don had frequently remarked that only 'Doctor Frost' would eradicate the fever, and that only when snow was visible on the distant mountains would the fever disappear. Bayly's description of Don gives a more sympathetic picture than do the anonymous carping critics quoted earlier. Although he refers to him earlier as 'poor old man,' he writes:

> Sir George Don, Lieut.-Governor and general in the Army, came from his cottage, in the southern part of the Rock, to the neutral ground thrice a week in his carriage, passing through some of the most unhealthy part of the town, yet he escaped the fever though in his 82nd year [sic]. He could read the smallest print without spectacles, and a more active, indefatigable old gentleman never existed...

The final death toll was over 1600, the highest since the first yellow fever epidemic in 1804.

The epidemic was over, but the squabbles of the medical profession rumbled on. Three committees to investigate the epidemic were set up. The Committee set up at the direction of Whitehall, on the advice of the Royal College of Physicians, was specifically to establish whether second attacks of yellow fever could occur in the same person. Don was instructed to preside over it, but delegated the job to Dr Pym, and the committee concluded (correctly) that second attacks of yellow fever occurred in the same patient very rarely, if ever. But the main arguments were between those who considered yellow fever to be contagious, and imported, and those who believed that it was not transmitted directly, and was domestic, occurring within the area because of insanitary conditions and 'bad air'. Most of the physicians already had entrenched views on this, and as a result the other two committees could come to no unanimous conclusions. The Anglo-French Commission, consisting of the three French physicians and Dr Barry, published the raw data only, without publishing its conclusions,[11] and the Army Medical Board's committee sat firmly on the fence, concluding, as George Don had, so many years before, that both quarantine and hygiene should be insisted on in any future epidemics.[12]

113

When a report appeared in the *Gibraltar Chronicle* on January 12th 1829 which gave the impression that General Don favoured the contagionist/importationist theory, this provoked an anonymous attack on Don published in *The Times*, and Don commented in a letter to England [13] 'I am well aware that there are in this Garrison persons disposed to find fault with my measures and who are not always influenced by a conscious adherence to the truth.' He added that he had been unaware of the article in question which had been published while he was very ill. The source of the original article was probably the PMO, William Pym, who was an ardent contagionist and importationist.

The Secretary of State to the Colonies, Sir George Murray, wrote to Don complaining that the Civil Hospital was being largely used by foreigners, and paid for by a tax on shipping. At Sir George Don's request, Hugh Fraser, Surgeon to the Civil Hospital, wrote a detailed report,[14] which Don forwarded to Murray, in which he remarked that the information supplied to Murray assumed that all patients with non-British names were foreigners, whereas in fact the vast majority were *bona fide* inhabitants of Gibraltar, most of whom indeed bore foreign names, and that the tax on shipping was only a minor part of the income of the Hospital, most of which was derived from contributions from the three religious persuasions, two of which represented the 'foreigners' complained of. He added that the figures quoted by Murray had not been sent in any official reports, and must have been supplied anonymously by an ill-wisher.

The attack on Don was continued in the medical journal *The Lancet*, which led the opposition to the contagionist/importationist view, [15] and the opinions expressed there are so similar to those in the poster campaign of 1828 as to suggest that the author was the same. The same journal returned to the attack in 1830,[16] with suggestions that Don and the various inquiries had been biased towards Pym's views.

The latter attack was preceded by two further anonymous reports to Sir George Murray. The first was about a private soldier who had died from a suspicious fever, and about alleged insufficient arrangements to prevent contagion. Replying to Murray's query,

Don remarked: '…some individuals write to their friends in London most infamous falsehoods respecting the Government.'

He included in his reply a report from Charles Farrell, the PMO, who stated that the disease was not yellow fever, and concluded 'is it not lamentable to find that their [the army medical officers] discussion on a single case of Disease, should be swelled into such importance as would seem to be implied by the tenor of your Excellency's letter?'

The second report which Don was called on to explain was of six cases of suspicious fever which had occurred in the Garrison. In fact, Don had already informed Murray of the precautions which he proposed to take in the summer season. In his reply to Murray, Don enclosed a report from Farrell that the cases were not contagious in his opinion. A month later, he was able to report that all cases had recovered, and that no further cases had appeared.[17]

In fact, Don's view had always been that he would take precautions against the yellow fever as if the two mutually exclusive theories were both correct.[18]

The report of the Director General echoes this, recommending good ventilation, attention to drains and sewers, and the avoidance of overcrowding, as well as strict quarantine regulations; and no criticism of Don's management of the epidemic is voiced in this report.[19]

At about the same time, anonymous reports appeared in *The Times* criticising various aspects of the appointment of Major Rowan as Civil Police Magistrate, the retirement of Howells, the previous magistrate, and the formation of the Court of Appeals. Don insisted that there had been no improper disclosures in Gibraltar. He commented that the reports 'emanate from the same anonymous source,' but did not think that they had originated in Gibraltar.

Who was responsible for the continued campaign against Don? It seems probable that it was a medical man, and a likely candidate is Peter Wilson, the Assistant Surgeon and Purveyor at the Civil Hospital, whom Don sacked in 1829 for going on leave without permission, after his leave had been cancelled so that he could testify before the Yellow Fever Commission. He settled in

Jerez, in Spain, and a few years later he was again making trouble for Gibraltar by spreading a false rumour that there was cholera in the Garrison.

All this criticism does not seem to have damaged Don's credibility with the Establishment. As we have seen, the Medical Director General of the Army had no criticism to make, and similarly, Sir George Murray does not seem have been affected by the appeal to him in *The Lancet*.

Murray does seem to have been less tolerant of Don's expenditure than Earl Bathurst had been, calling him to account for spending Crown money on the Garrison Library, and for the expenditure on furniture and repairs in the Convent and Governor's Cottage. Don replied to the latter complaint rather tartly,[20] saying that in the future he would himself pay for furniture and the salaries of various servants of what he referred to as 'Government House' (the Convent) and 'Government Cottage', to drive home the point that it was Murray's responsibility, not his, to pay for the upkeep of these establishments. Murray also implied that the figures of the census of 1829 were unreliable or even invented, as the total population recorded was exactly the same as in the previous census – 16394. He also suggested that Don was not being as zealous as he would have liked in keeping foreigners out. Don replied with detailed statistics, including a list of 380 foreigners expelled – mainly Spaniards.[21]

NOTES

1. Beauclerk, p. 322.
2. Don to Sir George Murray, Sept. 4th 1828. Governors Letters, GGA.
3. Anton, pp. 348-349.
4. Don to Hennen, Sept 8th 1828. Governors Letters, GGA.
5. Chervin, Vol. 1, pp. 390-392.
6. Jackson, Susan I.
7. Thornton.
8. Don to Murray. Governors Letters, November 30th 1828. GGA.
9. Don to Murray. Governors Letters, November 24th 1828. GGA.
10. Bayly, p. 277.
11. Chervin, passim.
12. McGrigor and Franklin.
13. Don to R.W. Hay. Governors Letters July 29th 1829. GGA.
14. Hugh Fraser to Don, Oct. 3rd 1829 (GGA)
15. Lancet, December 1829 pp. 455-456. (See Appendix III)
16. Lancet, Sept. 1830. pp. 31-32. (see Appendix III).
17. Don to Murray. 20th April 1830, 12th August 1830. Farrell to Don, 10th September 1830. Governors Letters, GGA.
18. Don to Bathurst, 29th Oct. 1814. Governors Letters, GGA.
19. McGrigor and Franklin.
20. Don to Murray, 4th November 1830. Governors Letters, GGA.
21. Don to Murray, 7th July 1829. Governors Letters, GGA.

Chapter 11

THE DONS AT HOME

One can get a fairly clear picture of George Don's character from the official record of his achievements. He comes over as conscientious and hard-working, and ever solicitous of the well-being of those under his command, whether soldiers or civilians. But there is relatively little information available about the private man, and even less about his wife, Maria Margaretta.

The Dons were childless, but their interest in education, and the numerous occasions on which they stood as godparents to the children of family and fellow-officers, must testify to their love of children.

One of the few existing non-official accounts of Don appears in the travel journals of Rose de Freycinet, her husband Louis, and the artist Jacques Arago.[1] They visited Gibraltar as their first port of call at the outset of a scientific mission led by Captain de Freycinet around the world on the corvette *Uranie*. They entered the harbour in November 1817, on the first French ship to anchor there since 1793. De Freycinet and his officers, accompanied by Mme. De Freycinet were presented to General Don by the French consul, Joseph Viale,[2] and were courteously received. His Excellency occupied an ancient building known as the Old Convent, richly furnished in the English manner, said de Freycinet, and ornamented with a number of pictures.

Arago, the artist, goes into more detail, describing one or two chairs of willow, an old oriental sofa, and a beautiful carpet.

...here is Arago's list of the works of art that met the Frenchmen's astonished eyes: the first, a basset hound, full-face; the second, a basset in profile; the third, a bulldog; the fourth, a greyhound; the fifth, a spaniel.[3]

Don's love of hunting is known, and he must have been a dog lover. It is probable that one of the reasons for his attempts to improve the roads in Spain was to make things easier for the Royal Calpe Hunt; he also provided kennels for the hounds at North Front.[4]

Also, it will be recalled that he was once fined for contravening the bye-laws of the Garrison Library committee – of which he was the President – for bringing his dog into the Library. One of the races at the racecourse in the Neutral Ground was for years afterwards known as 'the Don Mile,' and must have been endowed by him.

De Freycinet commented: 'General Don appeared to us to be of sound intelligence and a generous point of view, and to be devoted to the duties of his office.' Don showed great interest in the scientific aims of the voyage, and invited the party to see the sights of Gibraltar, regretting that he could not entertain them himself as his cook was at his country house (this was presumably his residence in the Spanish 'city' of San Roque).

George Don had an enquiring mind, and would therefore have been interested in the *Uranie's* world-wide scientific mission of exploration. In fact, at about the same time, another explorer actually named Cape Don, on the Cobourg Peninsula in the Northern Territory of Australia, after him.[5]

After the visit, a row broke out when the French Government wrote to their consul, Joseph Viale, alleging that Rose de Freycinet had gone ashore in male attire - the uniform of a French naval officer - and that this immodest behaviour had annoyed General Don. Viale replied that Mme. De Freycinet had in fact been dressed in civilian male dress (trousers and a frock coat), and that the General had received the party very cordially. However, Arago, in his account of the affair, recorded that the General's welcome had been cold, and his explanation about his cook being away seemed merely to be an excuse to avoid entertaining the party; he claimed that a member of Don's staff had confirmed this to him. However, he adds that Don 'in compensation' arranged for the party to go on a tour of the Galleries in the Rock, which Arago says was a courteous touch, as few strangers were allowed to see them. Whatever the truth of the matter, Rose resumed feminine attire, and there was no further trouble.

Many years later, in 1830, towards the end of Don's long career, the young Benjamin Disraeli visited Gibraltar on his way to a Grand Tour of the Mediterranean and the Holy Land.

119

We were presented by B.[6] to the Governor, Sir George Don, a
general and G.C.B., a very fine gentleman of the Windsor Terrace
school, courtly, almost regal in his manner, paternal, almost
officious in his temper, a sort of mixture of Lord St. Vincent and
the Prince de Ligne, English in his general style, but highly
polished and experienced in European society. His palace, the
Government House, is an old convent, and one of the most
delightful residences I know, with a garden under the
superintendence of Lady Don, full of rare exotics, with a beautiful
terrace over the sea, a berceau of vines, and other delicacies
which would quite delight you. Besides this, Sir George has a
delightful pavilion, modestly called the Cottage, at the extreme
point of the Rock, and a villa at San Roque, in Spain, about ten
miles off. Thus, by a constant change of residence, he counteracts
the monotony of his situation. He possesses a large fortune, all
of which he here disburses, and has ornamented Gibraltar as a
lover does his mistress. The Alameda here is superior to that at
Cadiz, with banks of pink geraniums, truly delicious. But Gibraltar
is a limited theatre for his Excellency, and he has civilised Spain
for twenty miles around, by making roads at his own expense,
building bridges, and reforming posadas. He behaved to us with
great kindness, asked us to dine, and gave us a route himself for
an excursion to the Sierra de Ronda...[7]

On Disraeli's return from Ronda, he was invited to dinner
with the Dons at Governor's Cottage.

We dined with the Governor at his cottage at Europa, a most
charming pavilion, and met a most agreeable party. Lady Don
was well enough to dine with us, and did me the honour of
informing me that I was the cause of the exertion, which though
of course a fib, was nevertheless flattering. She is, though very
old, without exception one of the most agreeable personages
that I ever met, excessively acute and *piquante*, with an aptitude
of detecting character, and a tact in assuming it, very remarkable.
To listen to her you would think you were charming away the
hour with a blooming beauty in Mayfair; and, though excessively
infirm, her eye is so brilliant and so full of *moquerie* that you
quite forgot her wrinkles. Altogether the scene very much
resembled a small German Court. There was his Excellency in
uniform covered with orders, exactly like the old Grand Duke of

120

Darmstadt, directing everything; his wife the clever Prussian princess that shared his crown; the aides-de-camp made excellent chamberlains, and the servants in number and formality quite equalled those of a Residenz. The repast was really elegant and *recherché* even for this curious age. Sir George will yet head his table and yet carve, recommend a favourite dish, and deluge you with his summer drink, half champagne and half lemonade. After dinner Lady Don rode out with the very pretty wife of Colonel Considine, and the man dispersed in various directions. It was the fate of Meredith [Disraeli's travelling companion] and myself to be lionized to some cave or other with Sir George. What a scene, and what a procession! First came two grooms on two barbs; then a carriage with four horses; at the window at which H.E. sits, a walking footman, and then an outrider, all at a funeral pace. We were directed to meet our host at the cave, ten minutes walk. During this time Sir G. tries one of the Arabians, but at the gentlest walk, and the footman changes his position in consequence to his side; but it is windy, our valiant but infirm friend is afraid of being blown off, and when he reaches the point of destination, we find him again in the carriage. In spite of his infirmity he will get out to lionize; but before he disembarks, he changes his foraging cap for a full General's cock with a plume as big as the Otranto one; and this, because the hero will never be seen in public in undress, although we were in a solitary cave looking over the ocean, and inhabited only by monkeys. The cave is shown, and we all get in the carriage, because he is sure we are tired; the foraging cap is again assumed, and we travel back to the Cottage, Meredith, myself, the Governor, and the cocked hat, each in a seat. In the evening he has his rubber, which he never misses, and is surprised I do not play 'the only game for gentlemen! You should play; learn.' However I preferred the conversation of his agreeable lady, although the charms of Mrs. Considine were puzzling, and I was very much like Hercules between – you know the rest.

Later, after he had left Gibraltar, Disraeli wrote to his father, asking him to send his latest novel to Lady Don:

While I remember it, a copy of the 'Young Duke' must be sent to Lady Don. Tell Ralph to attend to it. Write in the title 'Lady Don, by desire of the Author.' Enclose it to her, and then put another

121

cover, addressed to his Excellency. You will be surprised at me sending a light novel, and finding a muse in an old lady of seventy; but in truth she is the cleverest and most charming woman I ever met, beating all the Lydia Whites, Mrs. Weddells, and the Misses Bury out and out; and the only person I know who gives one the least idea of the Madame du Tencins and the other *brillantes*, who flirted with Hénault, chatted with Montesqieu, and corresponded with Horace Walpole. [9]

In these accounts we see the old General, cordial and hospitable, but always mindful of his dignity. An anonymous description of him as 'courtly in manner, and tenacious of the dress and ways of his earlier day,'[10] exactly fits Disraeli's account of the man.

Lady Don is the revelation. Throughout Don's career she is so much in the background as to be almost invisible. Disraeli's impression of her brings her to life – and what a character she must have been! Incidentally, in spite of the infirmity which Disraeli mentions, she survived into her nineties, and is buried in the English cemetery in Florence.

In fact, we know very little about her. She was an illegitimate daughter of Lord Elibank, who had no legitimate issue, but fathered a number of children, both before and after the death of his wife, by more than one mother. Maria Margaretta's mother is not known, but may possibly have been Mary Mortlock, of Kirtling in Cambridgeshire, who bore Lord Elibank several other children, including her sister Anne Murray, who is buried beside her in Florence, and two notable sailors of the time, James Mortlock, who discovered the Mortlock Islands in the Pacific, and Lewis, who was the hero of a sea battle in the Channel against the French, while he was commander of *HMS Wolverine*, as a result of which he perished.

It is surely no coincidence that Kirtling was the seat of the 6th Lord North, who had been the first husband of Lord Elibank's wife, Maria Margaretta de Jonge, after whom Lady Don was presumably named.[10]

The young Maria Margaretta must have been a favoured child. Unlike some of Lord Elibank's other illegitimate children, she took

122

her father's name of Murray, and he settled £5000 on her – a considerable sum in those days – when she married George Don. She must have been considered part of the family by her uncle General Murray, as she accompanied Lord Elibank's sister in law, the General's wife, to join him in Minorca, and seems to have been adopted by him, whether formally or not. General Murray, writing to William Young, another of Patrick's illegitimate children, says of her:

> You have a Sister who is adopted by us the very image of her Father, in Soul, and Feature, if you knew her you would envy the happiness Mrs. Murray and I have in so agreeable a Companion.[11]

Maria must have met Don in Minorca, while he was serving under Murray. She married him in England after the loss of Minorca, and was in Gibraltar with him in the 1790s. She went to Germany in 1795 to be with him there, accompanied by her sisters, when they underwent a dangerous passage across the North Sea.[12] She was with him in Jersey during his time as Lieutenant Governor – a letter from her survives in the archives of the Societé Jersiaise – and accompanied him on his journey to Walcheren.

During Don's tenure of the Lieutenant Governorship of Gibraltar, Maria Don is credited with the development of the garden of the Convent, their official residence, and she also took an interest in education, presenting the prizes at one of the schools which Don had founded. Her attendance at theatrical performances is recorded in the *Gibraltar Chronicle*.

Whenever there was a public subscription, her name appears on the list of contributors, always donating a modest amount compared to Don's munificent contribution, although she was certainly well off in her own right – both Lord Elibank and her uncle, the Hon. James Murray, had been generous to all their relatives, legitimate or otherwise, in their wills. It is almost as if she deliberately remained in the shadow of her husband, to avoid outshining him in any way.

Then comes Disraeli's description of her in her seventies. It makes us wish we knew more about her in her younger days.

NOTES

1. Bassett,. pp 11-15.
2. Joseph Viale, who was the brother of the more flamboyant Sir Emanuel Viale, was Consul for France in Gibraltar.
3. Bassett, p. 12-15; Arago, p. 23.
4. Fergusson, p. 3.
5. King.
6. This was Dr. Alexander Broadfoot, Inspector of Health at Gibraltar at the time.
7. R. Disraeli, pp.8-10. (Letter II).
8. Ibid. pp. 22-25 (Letter IV).
9. Ibid. pp. 55-56 (Letter VII)
10. Griffiths. I am grateful to Robert Griffiths for the information in the last two paragraphs; Murray, A.C, p. 183.
12. Manuscript annotation in the copy of Sullivan's *General Sir George Don, Lieutenant Governor of Jersey*, in the Scottish United Services Museum, Edinburgh.
13. Don Papers, Vol IV, f. 253 : Letter to Don from J Beaner in London:
    'I at once condole with you on the Hazards, and congratulate you on the Escape, of Mrs. Don and her sisters, on their passage to Cuxhaven, and I hope soon to hear, thro' my sister, that their Health has not suffer'd by the shock they have received.'

Chapter 12

THE FINAL YEARS

The years that followed the yellow fever epidemic were at first dominated by the deliberations of the Commissions of Enquiry, and the ongoing disagreements among the medical profession about almost every aspect of the disease.

In 1830, the new Charter of Justice was promulgated. Don, as Lieutenant Governor, was no longer the head of the system of justice. A Chief Justice was appointed [1] as head of the new Supreme Court, and the unwieldy system of the Charter of 1817, with several different Courts, was superseded.

A civil police force was established, with a Police Magistrate and a Chief of Police. This establishment is often quoted as the first police force in the British Empire outside the United Kingdom, coming into being shortly after the British police force established by Sir Robert Peel, but in fact the police in Gibraltar can be said to have been established much earlier. According to Montgomery Martin,[2] writing in 1835, 'The Police of Gibraltar owes its present existence, exclusively to his Excellency Sir George Don.' He is, of course, referring to the sanitary police force established in 1814, from which the present police force is directly descended.

1830 was a landmark date in the constitutional development of Gibraltar. With the establishment of a purely civilian judiciary, Gibraltar began to approach the status of a Crown Colony, rather than a garrison town - until then it was always referred to in official correspondence as 'the Town and Garrison of Gibraltar in the Kingdom of Spain', although in 1835 it was still possible to write that: '...the settlement is treated as a garrison town.'[3] It is not clear when Gibraltar officially became a colony, but from 1830, the Civil Secretary, who was the chief officer of the civilian government under the Governor, was more and more frequently referred to as the Colonial Secretary, although the two titles seem to have been used interchangeably for many years.[4]

125

In March 1831, Don received a dispatch from Viscount Goderich, the Secretary of State for the Colonies, informing him that he was to be replaced as Lieutenant Governor of Gibraltar. Although he must have been expecting this, it still came as a shock to him, and he wrote back to Goderich begging for an extension – even without pay, it seems:

I respectfully solicit from His Majesty as a Boon to which my long service and devoted attachment to His Royal Family may afford me some claim, that I may be permitted to remain in the exercise of this command until the Spring of 1832 to afford me time to make arrangements necessary for my future comfort in private life in the mean time. I should be satisfied with any pecuniary arrangements respecting my Income as Lieutenant Governor that His Majesty's Government may fix on.[5]

But Goderich was not to be moved, and Don was informed in April that he would be replaced in September by Major General Sir William Houstoun, a veteran of the Peninsular War.

Don was appointed Governor of Scarborough Castle, but he was never to leave Gibraltar to take up this honorary post. On January 1st 1832 he died of influenza at Line Wall House (now Duke of Kent House). One contemporary historian of Gibraltar claimed that he died of a broken heart at having to leave the work he loved.[6]

.... Two years subsequent to this unhappy occurrence [the yellow fever epidemic], Government determined on removing the Lieutenant Governor, who during seventeen years, with a short interval, had so ably conducted the affairs of this important fortress. To Sir George Don, who had identified himself with the Rock, and who hoped to die in office, this unexpected event produced much chagrin, and undoubtedly hastened his death.

George Don was buried with full military honours in the still unconsecrated new Protestant Church, where there is an impressive monument to him. The Gibraltar Chronicle of the 3rd January announced that the funeral would take place on the following day, 'if weather permits.' This unusual proviso, making the funeral depend on fine weather, was to allow for an extended funeral procession, to allow the people to pay their last respects to the man who had led them for so long and had so improved their lot. Although Line Wall

House is next door to the Church (now the Anglican Cathedral of the Holy Trinity), the funeral cortege travelled down the length of Line Wall Road as far as Montagu Bastion and back along the whole of Waterport Street, to the Church. Minute guns were fired during the length of the procession, and three rounds of eleven pieces of artillery were fired from the King's Bastion after the burial. The nearby towns of Spain joined in the general mourning; minute guns were also fired at Algeciras during the procession, and the Governor of Algeciras, General Monet, sent his two sons and aides de camp, as well as other officers, to the funeral.[7]

In his will, signed a few days after he had received the news that he was to be replaced, Don left everything to this wife. His possessions, which were auctioned off in Gibraltar in the weeks following the funeral, include three carriages and several horses, as well as furniture, books and a great variety of household objects, even including kitchen utensils.[8]

Lady Don must have left Gibraltar shortly after the funeral, probably to London, where the will was proved in April. When we next hear of her, she is in Italy; her solicitor in London replied on her behalf to a letter from the War Office, which in classical bureaucratic fashion was claiming repayment for some kitchen equipment that Don had bought for the Convent with public money – perhaps those very items which had just been sold at auction. Lady Don's solicitor assured the War Office that he would inform her of the claim on her return from Italy, where she had gone for some months for a rest. There is no indication that she ever returned, and one may be forgiven for hoping that the War Office is still waiting for its money.

Maria Margaretta Don seems to have settled permanently in Italy after the death of Sir George, whom she survived by more than twenty years. She died in 1854 at Villino Strozzi, just outside Florence, aged 91. She is buried in Florence, in the British cemetery at Piazza Donatello, where her grave is marked by a handsome marble pillar. Next to it there is an identical monument to Miss Anne Murray, her sister, who had died some years earlier at the age of 75. Miss Murray may have been Lady Don's companion for many years – even in Gibraltar; the subscription list for the Poor Fund

127

during the 1828 epidemic shows a donation of $100 from Lady Don, followed by a more modest $16 from Miss Murray.

Lady Don's will confirms that there was no issue of the marriage; her bequests are to the children of her relatives and friends, some of whom bear the names Maria Margaretta or George Don, indicating that the Dons had stood as their godparents. There is no mention of relatives of George Don in either of their wills; the Don line seems to have ended with him, unless John Don in Jamaica had descendants; their brother William had also died without issue in 1817.

NOTES

1. The first Chief Justice was Barron Field, a descendant of Oliver Cromwell, and a writer as well as a lawyer. As a young man he was a friend of Charles Lamb, and was a member of a group which included Wordsworth, Coleridge, Hazlitt and Leigh Hunt. He had been theatrical critic to The Times, advocate-fiscal of Ceylon, and Judge of the Supreme Court of New South Wales, where he was accused of encouraging litigation in order to augment his income. He returned to England in 1826 to resume his career at the Bar, but this did not prosper, and he was forced to apply for the new post of Chief Justice at Gibraltar. Disraeli took an instant dislike to him when they met in Gibraltar in 1830, and Field does not seem to have got on with Sir George Don, either. (See the article on Field in the Dictionary of National Biography).
2. Montgomerie Martin, p. 93.
3. Ibid. p. 91.
4. Personal communication: T.J. Finlayson, Gibraltar Government Archivist.
5. Don to Goderich. Governors Letters 17th March 1831. GGA.
6. Bell.
7. Bell, p. 193.
8. Gibraltar Chronicle, 4th January 1832.
9. Gibraltar Chronicle, Vol I, 1832, passim.

Chapter 13

SUMMARY

George Don's career divides itself naturally into two parts: From 1772 to 1806 he was an army officer on active service, and from 1806 to 1831 he was Lieutenant Governor successively of the island of Jersey and of the fortress of Gibraltar.

For nearly sixty years continuously he served Britain well, and if in the period of active service he won no outstanding battle honours, he was well enough thought of to advance to the rank of General, although other honours were slow in coming.

After the siege of Fort St. Philip in Minorca, his commander, General Murray, publicly commended him in a letter to Lord Hillsborough,[1] and showed his esteem in another more personal way - by giving his blessing to Don's marriage to his niece and ward.

During his first posting to Jersey, Don seems to have won the regard of the people, and regret was publicly expressed at his departure.

He took part in the unsuccessful campaign in Holland in 1793-1794. Subsequently he acted as Deputy Adjutant General to the army on the Continent and organised a spy network which brought in information from the territories under control of the French. Later on, he had another desk job, as Commissioner to the Prussian Army, and was later responsible for preparing the defences of the Isle of Wight against Napoleonic attack.

During the Helder campaign in 1799, Don commanded a brigade in the Duke of York's army, and by his own account was 'Publickly mentioned for his conduct in the action of the 19th September.'[2] This is the only occasion where we have evidence of a recognised success in the battlefield. However, this success was followed by a resounding failure - his capture by General Brune while on an undercover mission, which resulted in ten months of captivity as a prisoner of war.

129

Following his release he was put in charge of the troops in the Isle of Wight, and then posted to Scotland where, according to Miller,[3] he seems to have done a good job in making sure that the south-east of Scotland was well prepared to repel a possible French invasion.

In 1805, Don was placed in charge of a force which was to be sent to Germany, and at the same time he was also entrusted with some delicate diplomatic negotiations at the Prussian Court. However, he was replaced in both missions by more aristocratic figures (Lord Cathcart and Lord Harrowby), and in any case events elsewhere ensured that these enterprises would prove to be abortive.

All these years were George Don's period of active service, and if he had little opportunity to prove himself a dashing warrior, as contemporaries such as Sir John Moore certainly did, he was able to impress his superiors with his organisational ability and capacity for hard work. As a result he was sent to Jersey as Lieutenant Governor.

By his work in Jersey he consolidated his reputation as an efficient administrator, who was able to gain the confidence of a rather touchy populace, while carrying out his task of making the island safe from invasion, and, almost incidentally, making it a better place for that populace to live in. Ragg, in his book A Popular History of Jersey, writes:[4]

> there was sworn in as Lieut. Governor one whose name will always stand out as ``amongst the best of all,'' in the person of Lieutenant General Don, to whose untiring devotion and remarkable energy the Island owes the greatest of its improvements, and who certainly with regard to its roads, means of communications, and other conveniences, converted it from a wilderness into a decently inhabitable spot; besides taking care of its defences, and keeping always to the fore the bettering of the condition of its inhabitants.

All this could describe equally well Don's work in Gibraltar.

The Walcheren episode of 1809 served to underline Don's talent for organisation, as he struggled to achieve the repatriation of the ailing army, while arranging for the destruction of the port of Flushing to deny its use to the French.

Enough has been written in chapters five to twelve about George Don's work to improve Gibraltar; but a few 'before and after' comments from contemporaries will serve to highlight the enormous change for the better seen as a result of his efforts.

Dr. John Hennen had served in Gibraltar before Don's arrival, and was later his Principal Medical Officer, in the 1820s, until he succumbed to the yellow fever in 1828. He was thus in a good position to assess the improvements:[5]

> Within the town there formerly existed several spots remarkable for their filth, and for the crowded state of the inhabitants. Many of these places have been entirely new modelled; the low, ill-ventilated sheds, which incumbered the surface of the ground, have been removed; premises of a more permanent nature have been repaired, and greatly improved, and, in several instances, the whole of the former buildings have been razed, and edifices of a very superior character have been erected, insomuch, that persons who were familiar with Gibraltar before the epidemic of 1814 can now scarcely recognise many parts of it.

To be sure, many parts of Gibraltar, especially in the upper town, remained dirty and overcrowded throughout most of the 19th century,[6] but this only emphasizes how unspeakable the conditions must have been before the improvements which followed Don's arrival on the scene.

Colonal Bayly, who was in Gibraltar from 1828 to 1830, describes Don towards the end of his life:

> He could read the smallest print without spectacles, and a more active, indefatigable old gentleman never existed; in fact, Gibraltar owes all the beauties it possesses to his ingenuity and rage for improvement, which ultimately embellished the most sterile sand and rock with flowers and shrubs of infinite variety and beauty. [7]

A later Governor, Alexander Woodford, who visited Gibraltar as a young officer in the early years of the century, succinctly described the Gibraltar which he saw then as 'a dungheap,' [8] and Lord Nelson himself, shortly before his death at the Battle of

Trafalgar, is said to have described the Rock as 'this dark corner of the world.'[9] General Cockburn, who visited Gibraltar in 1810, wrote; 'The town of Gibraltar is very poor and miserable in appearance,'[10] and remarked that although the defences had been fully repaired since he had last been in Gibraltar – during the Great Siege – the barracks were much neglected. He also remarked on the number of cemeteries, which was not surprising after the terrible yellow fever epidemic of 1804.

Although Gibraltar in the early years of the nineteenth century is often described as 'prosperous' because of the flourishing entrepôt trade which came about as the result of the Napoleonic embargoes, the money earned went into relatively few pockets. The town itself had never been rebuilt after the destruction caused by the Spanish bombardment during the Great Siege, and accommodation was thus at a premium. Those who became rich as a result of the increase in trade had for the most part little interest in improving the lot of the common people, many of whom had gravitated to Gibraltar from other parts of the Mediterranean seeking to scrape a living in its buoyant economy. These unfortunates crowded into the town and had to pay exorbitant rents to live in insanitary and overcrowded huts and tenements.

The Committee of Public Health, formed during the 1804 yellow fever epidemic, was in no doubt as to the effects of this overcrowding: [11]

> ...the Town, not being sufficiently large to contain properly such an Encrease of population, has consequently been crowded to a degree unequalled and the avarice of House and Landholders, mostly aliens, has led them not only to erect Houses and Sheds in the most confined unhealthy Situations wherein to lodge those Strangers, but they have even let rooms to them by the Night in which they are assured that sometimes upwards of twenty have spent thereby infecting one another if disease happened to be among them which their filthy state was enough alone to generate.

The Committee of 1804 was of course selected exclusively from British officials and British merchants.

It was the influence of Don, a decade or more later, who recruited many of the successful 'alien' businessmen – no doubt including some of the slum landlords attacked by the author of the above quotation – into committees for the betterment of the town as a whole, which provided the stimulus towards civic responsibility which was an important factor in forging the Gibraltarian civil community.

From the many improvements which Don initiated, and which have been described in previous chapters, we may select two to illustrate this point: The imposition of rates on the business population for keeping the town clean may not have had immediate unanimous approval, but it made the middle class, at least, stake-holders in the town, with a Committee for Scavenging and Paving which was composed of civilians. Secondly, he did not just build the Civil Hospital, which in itself was a unifying force – he made sure that it was run, for the most part, by the civilian community. In fact, the term 'Gibraltarian' appears in writing for the first time, albeit in Latin, on the plaque commemorating the opening of this institution – `cives gibraltarienses'. It is not too fanciful to say that George Don presided over the dawn of the Gibraltarian identity which we are so proud of today. This was perhaps his greatest achievement.

It has been remarked by more than one historian that Don seems to have had no particular love for the Gibraltarians, whom he once referred to as 'a Class of people who, while they pretend to the Right, have not acquired the Sentiments of Englishmen,' [12] and he must sometimes have been irritated by obstacles placed in his path by some of the inhabitants, when his proposed reforms interfered with their short term interests; but this did not stop him from doing his best for them, in spite of their opposition. In this, he followed the precept which he was fond of quoting to the citizens of Jersey: *'Je vous ferai du bien malgré vous.'*

A modern Spanish historian[13] pays tribute to the effect Don had in fostering a civic consciousness among the Gibraltarians, and later comments that the prestige acquired by Sir George Don in Gibraltar was unequalled by any other Lieutenant Governor.

In many ways, Don foreshadowed the attitudes of the better Victorian Colonial administrators, and indeed, as we have seen, he was the mentor of one of them, Sir George Arthur, whose thirty year career took him to British Honduras, Canada, Tasmania and India.[14]

Let two American visitors to Gibraltar towards the end of George Don's reign have the last word:

> General Don, the present Lieutenant Governor, has grown old in the command of Gibraltar, and much of the neatness, general order, and discipline observable throughout the Garrison is attributable to his taste and activity. [15]

Washington Irving, perhaps the first American author to acquire an international reputation, has this to say:

> Sir George Don, the Governor of Gibraltar, is a fine compound of the veteran soldier, the keen sportsman and the old English country gentleman. He keeps up strict order in the garrison, all the military works are admirably perfected and maintained, he has turned the slopes and skirts of the once sterile and glaring rock into a delicious oriental garden...[16]

NOTES

1. Murray to Lord Hillsborough. Gentlemen's Magazine. 1782, Vol. 52, p. 161.
2. See Appendix I.
3. Miller.
4. Ragg, Ch. XXXI.
5. Hennen, p. 46.
6. Sawchuk, pp. 171 ff.
7. Bayly, p. 277. In the very next page, however, Bayly describes Gibraltar as 'that hotbed of vice, filth and disease, the barren rock of Gibraltar.'
8. Andrews. p. 140.
9. Ellicott, p. 20.
10. Cockburn, p. 17.
11. Sweetland, W. Quoted in Sawchuk, L.A. and Burke, S.D.A. Gibraltar's 1804 Yellow Fever Scourge: The Search for Scapegoats. Journal of the History of Medicine, Vol 53 pp. 29-30.

12. Don to Bathurst. Governors Letters, 17th January 1815. GGA.

13. Sepúlveda, pp. 187, 204.

14. Shaw, passim.

15. Anon (3). Vol. II. p. 257.

16. Irving. Vol II, p. 306.

Appendix I

The following letter, written in 1815, and the written statement from 1817, give Don's views on the failure of the Government to grant him a knighthood. Although he advances logical reasons why he is entitled to receive such an award, it was clearly a deeply felt personal matter for him.

To Sir Henry Bunbury, K.C.B.[1]

Gibraltar, 17th April 1815

My dear Sir,

    As I am aware that Lord Bathurst has been assailed on many sides by innumerable applications respecting the Order of the Bath, I should feel the greatest reluctance in obtruding myself on His Lordship's notice were I not urged by the repeated suggestions of my friends, and by a consideration of the high situation in which I have been placed here, to address His Lordship on this subject.

    I am not sure whether I ever mentioned to Lord Bathurst, or to yourself, that on my return from Walcheren I received from His Majesty's Ministers the most flattering approval of my conduct while in that command, and the late Mr. Percival promised he would recommend me for some Royal mark of Military favour and from what he stated to me, I have reason to believe that the Order of the Bath would have been conferred upon me at that time, had not very powerful interests been brought forward in favour of Lord Beresford.[2]

    As you have been in the Mediterranean I need not point out to you that in our commands we are in constant communication with Foreigners, and I assure you that Generals, particularly those possessing my Rank, are scarcely respected unless they are decorated with an Order.

    The Generals I have lately had communication with, both personally and by correspondence, have all Orders of the first class, and unfortunately, last November, in consequence of a letter from a Personage of the highest Rank, a report was propagated here, that I was created a Knight of the Bath.

This was circulated in Spain, France and in the Mediterranean, and shortly afterwards I actually received the congratulations of many Generals and other persons of distinction, on the honor conferred upon me.

When the new arrangement for the Order of the Bath came out and my name did [not] appear, it gave rise to many unpleasant remarks, and which even went so far as to produce conclusions that my conduct in my command here had not met with approbation, particularly as Maitland[3] was included, and also because his Government in the eyes of Foreigners is considered very inferior to mine.

I am quite sorry for having occupied your time by entering into this sort of detail, and trust Lord Bathurst, in the communication I have made to him on this subject, will perceive my motives have arisen from feelings connected with the high and important situation in which I have been placed, and the urgent suggestion of my friends.

I have the honor to be, with the greatest regards,
My dear Sir
Your most Obed[t.] humble Serv[t.]
Geo. Don [4]

P.S. I have this moment been informed that according to the new regulations of the Order, the Knights of the first Class are to be taken from those of the Second, but this of course would not affect me as in one Gazette I may be placed in the Second Class and in the next Gazette removed to the First Class.

G.D.

In 1817, George Don was awarded the Order of Military Merit of France by King Louis XVIII. Although the British Government had initially approved Don's acceptance of the award, Lord Castlereagh withdrew the permission, and Don wrote to Lord Bathurst, enclosing the following statement. Shortly afterwards he was finally allowed to accept the honour.

A copy of the statement is to be found in the Governors Letter Book for 1817 in the Gibraltar Government Archives. 30 July 1817.

Statement [By General Don]

That General then Colonel Don served with the Army under the Command of His Royal Highness the Duke of York and subsequently with General now Earl Harcourt in the years 1794 & 5 and acted for a considerable part of the time as Adjutant General, that this situation necessarily led him to frequent and close communication with the Princes of the Blood Royal of France who also served in that Army; that he was honoured with their confidence and that their acquaintance with his Zeal and exertions for their cause, the avowed object of which was the restoration of the House of Bourbon to its legitimate rights had created a friendship in their part towards him, which had been continued to him ever since, and which the distinguished mark of Favour, in conferring on him the Military Order of Merit of France must chiefly owe its source. To the nature of his Services with the Army, as giving him claim to the Order bearing such an appellation, General Don appeals with confidence to His Royal Highness the Duke of York, and of General the Earl of Cathcart.[5]

That General Don commanded a Brigade of the Army in Holland under the Orders of His Royal Highness the Duke of York in 1799, and that he was publickly mentioned for his conduct in the action of the 19th September.

That General then Lt General Don in consequence of his service, as above stated, was in the year 1805 entrusted with the Command of the Army which landed in the Elbe, that though the avowed object of this Force was not more than in later instance to co-operate with the Allies toward the restoration of the Bourbons, yet it was to lend its aid to oppose and overthrow the Usurper of their Throne.

That the Services of General Don in 1813 in the Island of Jersey, as connected with the cause of the Bourbons, was purely of a Military nature, in which he had the honor of acting in concert with his Royal Highness the Duke of Berry.[6]

138

It may be remarked that services in the field as relating to the French King, can only refer to such services, performed in the common cause against Revolutionary France. The British Armies even down to the Battle of Waterloo never having fought declaredly for the Royal cause; and that General Don having as above stated actually served in the field, with the Royal Family of France, and when the Royal Cockade appeared there, has a more peculiar claim to any mark of his Most Christian Majesty's favour.

NOTES

1. Governors Letters (GGA). Major General Sir Henry Bunbury (1778-1860) was at the time Under Secretary for War. He had served in the Duke of York's staff at the Helder with Don, who seems to have been friendly with him, and wrote a book about that campaign. He had been awarded the KCB in 1814.

2. Viscount Beresford (1768-1854) received the Order after the Battle of Busaco, where he had distinguished himself by organising and leading the Portuguese forces in that successful campaign. He was highly regarded by Wellington, who was probably one of the 'powerful interests' which Don mentions. Even if he had not had such an influential supporter, it is understandable that the Government would have preferred to give the vacant Order to a hero of a successful battle, rather than to Don, who had done sterling work in retrieving the forces from Walcheren – a campaign which the Government surely did not want the public to be reminded of! Spencer Percival has the distinction of being the only British Prime Minister to have been assassinated, and when this occurred in 1812 Don must have felt that his chances of a knighthood had diminished even further.

3. Sir Thomas Maitland (1759?-1824) was Governor of Malta at the time the letter was written. In December 1815, he was made Commander- in-Chief of the whole Mediterranean (excluding Gibraltar) – a promotion which must have caused Don even greater annoyance.

4. This letter was written in Don's own hand, in triplicate, as was a similar letter of the same date to Lord Bathurst.

5. The 2nd Earl of Cathcart was Quartermaster General at the time. He had served in the Walcheren Expecdition, and was disabled for a long time from the effects of the Walcheren Fever. Later, he fought at the battle of

Barossa, and at Waterloo, where he had three horses shot from under him.

6. It is not clear what service Don did for the French Royal Family in 1813. He may have helped the Duc de Berry to travel to France in 1814, after Napoleon's banishment to the island of Elba. The Duc de Berry (1778-1820) was the 2nd son of the Comte de Artois, who later became King of France as Charles X. Whatever it was, the Duc must have been grateful -he presented Don with a double- barrelled flintlock sporting gun, with silver inlays, which is now in the National Museum of Scotland in Edinburgh.

Appendix II

The following letter, from the Governor's Letter Book in the Gibraltar Government Archives, gives Don's very detailed analysis on what he considered were essential requirements for the defence of Gibraltar. It is also quite revealing of Don's attitude to the Gibraltarians, the Spanish – and to his own troops.

Don to Lord Bathurst
Duplicate
Gibraltar 6 July 1816

Secret

My Lord,

I have had the honor to receive your Lordship's letter of the 30th of May (marked private) the contents of which demand the most mature consideration.

In calculating the Force which should comprise the Peace Establishment of this Garrison, consistently with the Safety of the Place, the following points must be duly attended to.

1st. The Northern Front

The Front, although narrow and strong by nature against the regular approaches of a Besieging Army, is unquestionably defective in many points, particularly in the means of resistance against a sudden attack of Infantry. The Post at Bay-side in its present state cannot resist the attack of a storming Column above a few minutes, and communication would then be opened to the Glacis at Land port, with the trifling exception of a Barrier Gate lately placed across the Causeway, and as there are no proper outworks the Covert way would soon be carried. There never being a sufficient Garrison to defend it with Infantry, consequently the Defence must depend on Artillery and your Lordship is aware of the time it requires to bring heavy Ordnance into effect, and how far a column by a rapid movement might penetrate in a dark night before that could be done.

The possession of the Covert-way with Waterport Ditch cuts off the interior works of the Water-port Front from the body of the Place, and the enemy will then have the means of escalading

141

the Scarp Walls of the Curtain of the Grand Battery, North Bastion, Waterport Curtain, Montague Bastion and the Curtain between Montague and Orange Bastion.

The post at Lower Forbes, in consequence of the Wet Ditch in its Front, is capable of some defence and the passage of the Orillon Ditch may also be defended for some time.

Your Lordship will perceive by what I have already stated, that the North of the Land Front of this Garrison is only one single line of Works, hence the absolute necessity of guarding against surprise even in time of the most profound Peace.

I do not by any means wish to find fault with the Works which have been constructed within the last twenty-six years on the Water-port Front, but I must deeply lament that the North Front has not been taken into consideration and strengthened, as upon the defence of it against a sudden attack from the Land side, the security of the Body of the Place depends; as the moment an Enemy has, as I have already stated, carried Land-Port Covert-Way and occupied the Ditches, all the exterior works of the Waterport Front are cut off and taken in reverse and the other works in the Quarter exposed to escalade.

I have not mentioned the two Places of Arms on the North Front, as neither could hold out after the Covert-Way is carried

I find that great reliance has been placed upon the effect of Artillery in the defence of the North Front, but I humbly beg to differ in opinion with those who place so great a reliance on that Arm under the foregoing circumstances.

A surprise attack can only be attempted during the night, and that possibly in bad Weather, the manning of the great guns is an operation of some time and after the guns are completely brought into action, their fire is slow and uncertain when directed upon a moving object, and when the Enemy has reached the Ditch none but flanking guns can act, and from the bad construction of the Flanks their fire would be very ineffectual. I therefore consider it very extraordinary that some exterior works have never been constructed on this front (in fact the most vulnerable quarter) to arrest the progress of an Enemy in his approach to the Body of the Place.

Two Casemates Redoubts, one at Lower Forbes and the other at Bay-side, and two demi-counterguards and one Bastion on Land-port-Glacis, would have rendered the North front of the Garrison extremely difficult to approach, either by regular operation or sudden attack. Water you command, and the lines on the right would afford an inaccessible and most excellent flank against the enemy's operations.

In time of War an attempt may be made to surprise the Garrison not only on the North and Water-port Fronts, but also along the whole extent of the Line Wall from the back of the Old Mole to Rosia Bay inclusive, but in time of Peace I consider it impracticable for the Spaniards to assemble without its being known a flotilla in this neighbourhood sufficiently numerous to take part in an attempt to surprise the Place. The Army in Spain, including the Militia, at this moment although ill paid and ill clothed, is yet efficient, and I am confident that a force of 30,000 men could be collected in the neighbourhood in the course of a very few weeks; but as long as the present Government exists I think there is no danger of attack from that Quarter, but here is a question, how long will the Spanish Government exist?

The People are certainly averse to the present Government, and all Ranks speak openly of its Impotency. When they lose their Colonies in South America, which I believe will very shortly happen I am sure that a few Men of Abilities would bring about a Revolution in Spain. In the first instance the whole Population would divide and attach themselves to the two Parties now existing viz. Los Serviles and Los Liberales. The moment Civil War broke out Armies would instantly be assembled in Andalusia and in this province the Liberales would no doubt prevail; would it then not be a great object for them to surprise Gibraltar? By the possession of it they would obtain a Place of Arms and Warlike stores of any kind for their future operations, besides which, the achievement would in itself be popular, and give them a powerful influence over all Spain. It is here necessary to mention that either the Serviles or the Liberales would at any time break the most solemn treaties, and make any sacrifice to obtain possession of the Place. I positively know that

143

even at this moment when the country is sunk so low the feelings of the Spaniards with respect to Gibraltar remain steadily the same.[1]

2nd. The Population of the Town.

I enclose for your Lordship's information a General Return of the Civil Inhabitants, by which you will perceive that the total Number amounts to 11,424 Persons, of this there are only 1117 British, 2248 Natives (Roman Catholic) and 770 British and Native Jews, making only 4195 Inhabitants who may be considered as belonging to and attached by interest to the British Government.

Your Lordship will perceive that there are 2,742 Spaniards, 1,818 Genoese and 1,312 Portuguese making of those countries 5,872, and there are other Foreigners who have no interest in our welfare, and consequently cannot be depended upon; besides which the average Population on board Vessels in the Bay amounts to 2000 Persons of which number the greatest proportion are Roman Catholic Foreigners and connected with those in Power.

These Foreigners, it is true, are not provided with any Military Arms, but according to the habits and customs of their Countries, there is not one of them without a knife, and your Lordship must be aware that the Portuguese, Spanish and Italians are extremely expert in the use of this Weapon, and are all addicted to the crime of assassination, and therefore might by a previous understanding with a foreign Power add considerably to an attempt to carry the place by surprise; indeed, I believe your Lordship will find in your own office a communication from the Minister at Lisbon on this subject, about the year 1808.

3rd. The Want of a Citadel.[2]

Your Lordship must be well aware that in all Garrison Towns there is a Citadel which is situated as not only to take part in the defences of the Place, but also to command and controul the People of the Town; this is not the case in Gibraltar, and therefore, the Civil Population here can only be kept in check by Infantry.

4th. The Distribution of the Force.

I am sorry to be under the necessity of observing to your Lordship that the situation of the Barracks does not at present accord with the defence of the Place. In the Town District two thirds of the

144

whole Force should be quartered, and in the South one third, whereas at present the Barracks accommodation only admits of one regiment being quartered in Town, and the other three are stationed in the South.

Casemates Barracks of 1500 men (these Casemates are constructed for 1500 men during a siege, but at other times a Regiment 1000 strong should be quartered in them) were commenced adjoining the Rampart of the Grand Battery on the North Front in the year 1809 and they are now in a great state of forwardness and almost ready for the turning of the Arches, but most unfortunately the Commanding Engineer has lately received instructions to lessen the expenditure for this year, which prevents his going on with this important work as rapidly as the additional number of Workmen lately arrived led us to expect.[3]

No orders have yet been received from the Treasury for the repair of the Town Range Barracks, so that the Barracks accommodation in the North District will inevitably diminish in the course of the ensuing winter.

The repairs and additions to the Windmill Hill Barracks I have most strongly recommended, as they are at all times essentially necessary on account of the health of the Troops,[4] and indispensable in time of war for the accommodation they afford.

6th. Roman Catholic soldiers Comprising Part of the Present Garrison.

I have already stated to your Lordship that the number of Civilians of the Roman Catholic persuasion within the limits of the Garrison and afloat amounts to 10,517 and I find by the returns which I have received from the several Corps, that the number of Roman Catholics including Officers, Sergeants, Drummer and Rank and File amounts at present to about 141 making a total of about 12,000. Were these soldiers employed where they could alone connect themselves with British Subjects I should not apprehend any mischief arising from their being of the Roman Catholic persuasion, but in this Garrison, where the bulk of the Population is composed of Foreigners who cannot be considered as interested for the present Possessors, it is certainly a circumstance which should not pass unnoticed.

145

7th. Duty of the Troops of the Line.

I most perfectly agree with your Lordship that it is essentially necessary towards preserving the health of the Soldier in this Climate that he should never have less than three nights in bed, and notwithstanding my having reduced the guards as low as possible consistently with the security of the Place and the preservation of good order, it was not until the arrival of the 5th Battalion of the 60th Regiment that I accomplished this great object, and even now, when the guards are more reduced than they have been at any former time, the Rank and File have only three nights in bed and sometimes four, by a reference to the returns this may not appear correct it is therefore necessary I should mention that a larger proportion of Rank and File is employed as Artificers and constant Labourers in the several Departments. I have used my best endeavours to reduce the number, but the Wages of Civilians are so high that I could not consistently with economy avoid employing the Troops.

The wages of a Soldier Mechanic are only nine pence per diem, whereas those of a Civilian average from five to seven shillings per diem.

I am well aware that it would be highly improper of me at the present moment to recommend the construction of the Works on the North Front of the Garrison which I here alluded to in the first part of this letter, however that casemated Redoubts would certainly afford great security against surprise and I think they should be constructed as soon as circumstances permit.

At present the effective Rank and File of the four Corps of the Line amount to 3,354, from which must be deducted the Average Sick viz. 200 men, and 392 Recruits at Drill, who do no duty, leaving 2762 Rank and File (which certainly is not excessive when the Line of Defence is upwards of four Miles in extent) to do all the Garrison duty, to furnish Artificers and constant Labourers, as well as daily workmen to the different Departments, and also to do all Regimental duties and work.

With regard to the Royal Artillery the effective number of Corporals, Bombardiers, and Gunners now here amounts to 344 Men; their labour as Artillerymen is constantly great, besides which

146

they have seldom above two nights in bed and sometimes only one, therefore it is very adviseable that an additional Company should be sent here in the month of October next.

The Companies of the Royal Sappers and Miners only consist of 210 Rank and File and all entirely employed as Artificers in the Engineer Department. This Corps does not take any share of Garrison duty.

I have already stated that the effective Rank and File of the Corps of the Line now in the Garrison (including Sick and Recruits at Drill) amount to 3,354 Men, and under all circumstances I am humbly of the opinion that this force should not be reduced until the Casemates at the Grand Battery are finished, the repairs to the Town Range Barracks completed, and the North Front entirely reformed; a Peace establishment of 3000 effective Rank and File of the Line might then be considered as a sufficient Force for the security of the Place.

I have the honor to be
My Lord
Your Lordship's
Most Obedient Humble Servant

Geo. Don
Gen¹.

P.S. The Return of the Population will be sent as soon as a duplicate Copy can be made out.

G.D.

NOTES

1. With Napoleon safely incarcerated in St. Helena, Whitehall was evidently trying to cut down on the expenditure of the military establishment at home and overseas. Don is concerned to maintain and even increase his forces in Gibraltar. He makes the point that the Spanish Government is unstable, and any party to a revolution there might find both strategic and political advantage in seizing Gibraltar, making the additional and

still valid point that whether at peace or war, as enemies or allies, the attitude of Spain to the British in Gibraltar had never changed.

2. Don no doubt remembered Jersey, where he was responsible for the completion of the great citadel of Fort Regent.

3. Casemates Barracks were in fact completed in the following year, but works continued around the Grand Battery for several years, so the Casemates Gate bears the name of Lord Chatham.

4. It had been noted during the yellow fever epidemic that inhabitants and troops who resided in the North Front or the Europa and Windmill Hill area to the South did not get the fever.

Appendix III

Following the yellow fever epidemic in Gibraltar in 1828, the influential medical journal *Lancet* printed the following reports from Gibraltar. The fulsome praise of Dr Nicolas Chervin in the first article stamps the author as an anti-contagionist and anti-importationist, and the terms of his criticism of Sir George Don suggests that he may have been the author of the anti-Don poster campaign in Gibraltar during the epidemic. *The Lancet* itself betrays its bias toward Chervin's opinions by the phrase 'the late endemic fever in Gibraltar' and confirms it in the final paragraph of the second piece.

The first report appeared in December 1829:[1]

LITERARY INTELLIGENCE

M. Chervin, member of the Legion of Honour, Doctor of Medicine of the faculty of Paris, already celebrated in Europe, by his exertions in investigating the causes of yellow fever, and other contagious disorders, has nearly completed a very voluminous work, reaching to five quarto volumes, on the late endemic fever in Gibraltar. He has brought forward a great mass of interesting matter, which seems finally to determine the question of contagion or non-contagion in favour of those who advocate the local origin of the disease. This work will be replete with extraordinary documents, some of which seriously implicate the conduct of the local government of that garrison, but more especially that of two of the principal medical officers, who, it would appear, were not over scrupulous in modifying the evidence and controlling the testimony of the witnesses. How these gentlemen will defend themselves from the inferences necessarily arising from the perusal of these papers remains to be seen; the reports of nearly all the British medical officers tend strongly in favour of Dr. Chervin, and upon these the public will be required to form their opinions.

If Dr. Chervin succeed in establishing his position, that the fevers which have so often desolated the south of Europe, and the West Indies, are of sporadical origin, the cumbrous quarantine machinery which has so long proved a source of expense to governments, and of embarrassment to commerce, must necessarily fall to the ground, in spite of the exertions of interested

149

individuals, however iniquitous may be their measures. It is to be regretted, that the cares of so important a government as that of Gibraltar, should be allowed to weigh down the declining years of that respectable but superannuated veteran, Sir George Don. When a functionary has become too old to perceive with his own senses, or to judge with his own understanding, he immediately becomes liable to be imposed upon by designing people, and acts of partiality and injustice necessarily arise. Had the worthy old General been in possession of his faculties, a meritorious officer could never have been subjected to a series of petty insults and oppressions, and finally to the deprivation of his office, merely because he had the honesty and independence to declare his sentiments, regardless of hints from head quarters.

In the work of Dr. Chervin,[2] the means of appreciating the conduct of every individual engaged in that melancholy scene will be afforded; and the Right Honourable Secretary for the Colonies, will be enabled to distinguish those individuals who have really done their duty, from those wretches who have wrought out their own interest at an enormous and appalling expense of human misery.

Strong stuff!

In fact, the main document published by the French physicians and Dr. Barry, published in Paris in 1830 in two volumes, confined itself to reporting facts, and not to apportioning blame.

The second report appeared in the *Lancet* for September 1830:[3]

RE-APPEARANCE OF THE YELLOW FEVER AT GIBRALTAR
[from a Correspondent.]

I have been favoured with a letter from Gibraltar, dated the 12ᵗʰ of August, of which the following is an extract:-

'The month of July has been unusually warm, and the heat at present continues very oppressive, the thermometer ranging as high as ninety degrees (Fahrenheit) in the shade. Some well-marked *sporadic* examples of the *autumnal bilious intermittent yellow fever* have appeared, and given rise to apprehensions little short of that existed previous to our fever of 1828 assuming its epidemic character. It is very remarkable that the Company of Sappers and Miners in the barracks on Hargrave's Parade, the locality where the first cases of the disease discovered itself in that year, are, as yet, the chief sufferers; and have, during the last week, sent *eight cases* to hospital, four of which exhibit *yellow skin*, and other combinations of symptoms which mark this *Protean* form of fever; in consequence of which, His Excellency, the governor (General Sir George Don), has ordered this corps to evacuate the barracks, and to occupy the sheds on the neutral ground; but whether these cases are to be considered the presage of future evil, I know not; neither shall I pretend, at so early a period of the season, to offer an opinion, although, borne out by three or four cases which have been admitted to the Civil Hospital, it would not, perhaps, be thought presumptuous in me to hazard one. However, something appears to be decidedly wrong at head-quarters; for Sir George has said, ``that he cares not a *damn* for the opinions of any military medical man in the garrison! That they know nothing at all about the disease!!'' Whether we are to argue from this, that our principal medical officer (Dr. Farrell), 'who, to use the words of Ben Johnson, ``no sordid hope of gain, or frosty apprehension of danger, could turn a parasite to time, place, or opinion,'' has said any-thing hostile to the ``importation'- and-contagion'' creed of our worthy General, I cannot say...[1]

The Lancet commented on the above report:

We refrain, for the present, from making any lengthened comments on the above extract, which, however, the importance of the subject would almost compel us to do, but will content ourselves quietly to await the course of events; and should our next intelligence from Gibraltar discover the cases remarked on by our correspondent to have assumed an epidemic character, we most sincerely trust that the enlightened secretary for the colonies, General Sir George Murray, will immediately cause to be dispatched to that fortress, a few well-educated medical men of tried integrity, and possessing sufficient rank to prevent the repetition of such hole-and-corner work as took place at the close of the epidemic of 1828. We need not remark, because it is sufficiently known, that the gallant secretary above alluded to, caused to be instituted a board of inquiry into the origins of that epidemic; but owing to the interested motives of some of the members of the board, together with the prepossessions of others, the intentions of the gallant secretary had well nigh been frustrated; and frustrated they would have been (for truth was

151

most clearly not the object sought by the majority of the board), had not the unbending integrity of Colonel Chapman and Judge Stowell,[4] two of the members, protected the opinions of the obviously conscientious, from the insolent and ignorant, cross-examinations of two men, who, most unceremoniously, were foisted into the commission, as we have good reason to know, without the honourable secretary ever being consulted on the occasion. For our own part, we have no wish to see any further examination instituted into the origin of this fever; for we have long considered all such fevers to be just as much the product of the soil as the potatoe; but it is just and proper, that so long as individuals are found arguing for an exotic origin of the distemper, that inquiry should be allowed to take place; and in such an inquiry it is most especially requisite that no persons who may be avowedly interested in support of this latter opinion be permitted to interfere, without having, at all events, their designs and movements submitted to the most rigid public scrutiny.

The Lancet and its correspondent must have been disappointed when no epidemic broke out in 1830. it was not until much later that the question was finally settled: both sides were wrong – the disease is not directly contagious, being transmitted only by a mosquito-bite, and in the case of Gibraltar at least, each epidemic was almost certainly imported from the West Indies.

NOTES

1. The Lancet, Dec 1829, pp. 455-456. Don reported these cases to Sir George Murray on August 12, 1830, enclosing a report from Dr Farrell, the Principal Medical Officer, who stated that the cases were of the normal seasonal diarrhoea, and were not contagious, although some of the symptoms were worrying. On the 10th September, Don wrote again, enclosing a further report from Dr Farrell: All six cases had recovered, and there had been no further cases.

2. Chervin et al.

3. The Lancet, Sept. 1830, pp. 31-32.

4. The Minutes of the Commission of Inquiry, (in the Gibraltar Government Archives), show that Chapman and Stowell (neither of them medical men) voted for the 'non-importation, non-contagion' opinion favoured by the *Lancet* and its Gibraltar correspondent, which probably accounts for the high praise lavished on them. Whether, in fact, they acted as

152

the *Lancet* describes is difficult to tell at this remove, but there can be little doubt that the medical members of the Commission must have been strongly influenced by Dr William Pym's strong contagionist and importationist views.

Bibliography

MANUSCRIPT AND ARCHIVE MATERIAL
British Library:
Don Papers; Add. Ms.46702-46711, 46883, 46884.
Cambridge University Library
Correspondence of the British and Foreign Bible Society.
Gibraltar Government Archives
Governors Letters, 1814-1831
Military Secretary's Letters, 1814-1831.
Diary, 1786 and 1787.
Ms. *Fever at Gibraltar: Conclusions of the Director General [Sir James McGrigor] and the Principal Inspector [Dr W Franklin] on the Findings by the Army Board of Enquiry on the 1828 Epidemic of Yellow Fever in Gibraltar.*
Minutes of the Commission of Enquiry
Gibraltar Garrison Library
Ms*: My Recollections.* by Capt. Henderson
Ms. Memoir by John Drinkwater, in his book of letters received by him from prominent people.
Typescript: *Holy Trinity Cathedral.* by DH Simpson.
Public Records Office
Colonial Office Papers: CO 91/61-68; WO 55/808.
Societé Jersiaise Library
Pamphlets and Miscellaneous Papers
Scottish United Services Museum and other Scottish archives
Manuscript annotation in copy of *General Sir George Don,* by J Sullivan, Jersey, 1884
Grant of Arms, 1810 to General George Don.
Marriage Settlement between George Don and Maria M Murray in Scottish records Office (GB2/250).
Anderson family tree in Anderson House, Fife. Courtesy of Stephen Aynscough.
Wellcome Institute Library
Ms: *Remarks on Occurrences at Gibraltar, 1828.* by William Thornton.

154

MAGAZINES, JOURNALS AND WEBSITES

Balfour, CB. 'Notes on Newton Don,' in *History of the Berwickshire Naturalists' Club,* Vol XIV, part 2, 1893.

Gazette de l'île de Jersey, 20th April and 25th May1793.

Gentleman's Magazine, 1782, Vol 52.

Gibraltar Chronicle, 1814-1832.

Isle of Wight Mercury, 25th June and 2nd July 1890.

Journal of the Cambridge Family History Society. May 2003: 'Virtute Fideque,' by RJH Griffiths, revised in Mortlock website (*http://www.mortlock.info*)

Journal of the History of Medicine, Vol 53

Lancet, Dec. 1829 and Sept. 1830.

Taezner, M: King's German Legion website: (*kgl.co.de*)

United Services Journal, 1832,.

Website: *http:/outworld.cs.com/kenseton2/Barnesline.htm*

BOOKS AND PAMPHLETS:

Amiel, R. *Answers to Queries from the Army Medical Board, on the Epidemic in Gibraltar, 1828.* London, 1829.

Andrews, A. *Proud Fortress,* Evans Bros,1958.

Anon. *Journal of a Tour in Italy in 1821, with a Description pf Gibraltar, by an American.* New York, 1824. (1)

Anon. *Upon this Rock.* Gibraltar, 1969. (2)

Anon. *A Year in Spain, by a Young American.* London, 1831. (3)

Anton, JA. *Retrospect of a Military Life.* Edinburgh, 1841.

Arago, J. *Voyage autour du monde.* Ardant, Limoges. No date.

Bailey, JW. *The Curious History of Dr Marshall.* Cambridge, Mass., 1930.

Balleine, Rev. GR. *Biographical Dictionary of Jersey.* Staples Press, London and New York, 1948.

Bassett, M. *Realms and Islands.* OUP, London, 1962.

Bayly, Col. *Diary of Colonel Bayly, 12th Regiment.* London, 1896.

Beauclerk, W. *Journey to Marocco.* London, 1828.

Beijnen, G. *De twee zendingen van den Generaal Don...in 1799.* Leyden, 1900?

[Bell, J] *The Traveller's Handbook of Gibraltar...by an Old Inhabitant.* Cowie, Jolland, 1844. (1)

Bell, J. *History of Gibraltar.* Pickering, 1845. (2)

Benady, S. *Civil Hospital and Epidemics*. Gibraltar Books, Grendon, 1994.

Benady, T. *Aaron Cardozo, Life and Letters*. Gibraltar Books, Grendon, 2004.

Borrow, G. *The Bible in Spain*. Ward Lock, 1842.

Caldelas Lopez, R. *Gibraltar en San Roque*. Caja de Ahorros de Cádiz, 1982.

Calderon Quijano, J. *Las fortificaciones de Gibraltar*. Sevilla, 1968.

Caruana, C. *The Rock under a Cloud*. Silent Books, 1989.

Chervin, N. *et al. Documens recueillis par MM Chervin, Louis et Trousseau, members de la commission Francais envoyée à Gibraltar pour observer l'épidémie de 1828; et par M le Dr Barry, médecin des armées anglaises*. Paris, 1830.

Cockburn, G. *Journey from Cadiz to Malaga*. London, 1815.

Davies, W. *Fort Regent, a History*. Jersey, 1971.

Dictionary of National Biography. OUP, 1885; *Oxford Dictionary of National Biography*. OUP, 2005.

Disraeli, R [Ed]. *Home Letters Written by the Late Earl of Beaconsfield*. John Murray, London, 1885.

Draper, Sir W. *Observations on General Murray's Defence*. London, 1783.

Ellicott, J.T. and Ellicott, D.M. *An Ornament to the Almeida: The History of Gibraltar's City Hall*. 2nd. Edition, 1993, Gibraltar Heritage Trust.

Fergusson, G. *Hounds are Home*. Springwood Books, London, 1979.

Finlayson, C. [Ed] *Gibraltar, 100 Years of Images*. Government of Gibraltar, 2004.

Ford, R. *Handbook for Spain,* London, 1845. (1966 edition).

Fortescue, the Hon. J. *History of the British Army*. Macmillan, 1902.

Gibraltar Directory and Guidebook for 1930. Gibraltar Garrison Library Printing Press, 1930.

Gilbard, GJ. *A Popular History of Gibraltar*. Garrison Library, Gibraltar, 1885.

Gwyther Jones, B. *Marble Hauls*. Weymouth, 1999.

Hennen, J. *Sketches of the Medical Topography and Diseases of the Mediterranean.* Underwood, London, 1830.

Hills, G. *Rock of Contention.* Robert Hale, 1974.

Hylton, Lord. *The Paget Brothers, 1790-1840.* John Murray, 1918.

Inglis, H. *Spain in 1830.* London, 1851.

Irving, PM. *The Life and Letters of Washington Irving,* Philadelphia, 1862.

Jackson, Gen. Sir W. *The Rock of the Gibraltarians.* Gibraltar Books, Grendon, 1987.

Jackson, Susan I. *Methodism in Gibraltar and its Mission to Spain, 1769-1842.* Thesis; University of Durham, 2000.

Kelaart, EF. *Flora Calpensis.* Ivan Voorst, London, 1846.

King, PP. *Narrative of a Voyage of Discovery...between the years 1818-1822.* John Murray, London, 1827.

Lawrance, C. *History of the Old Naval Hospital, Gibraltar.* Lawrance, Lymington, Hants, 1994.

Lempriere, W. *A Tour from Gibraltar to Tangier...Including a Particular Account of the Royal Harem.* London, 1783.

Luna, J.C. de. *Gibraltar ante las armas, la diplomacia y la política.* Madrid, 1952.

Mahon, R.H. *Life of General the Hon. James Murray.* John Murray, London, 1921

Miller, J. *History of Dunbar.* Dunbar, 1859.

Montero, F.M. *Historia de Gibraltar.* Cádiz, 1860.

Montgomerie Martin, R. *History of the British Colonies. Possessions in Europe. Gibraltar.* London, 1835. (Facsimile edition, Gibraltar Books, 1998).

Murray, A.C. *The Five Sons of 'Bare Betty.'* John Murray, London, 1936.

Oman, C. *Sir John Moore.* Hodder and Stoughton.

Ompteda, Baron. *A Hanoverian English Officer.* London, 1892.

Plá, J. *Gibraltar.* Hollis and Carter, 1955.

Quayle, W. *A General View of the Agriculture...of the Islands on the Coast of Normandy.* London, 1815.

Ragg, the Rev. A E. *A Popular History of Jersey.* 1896
Report on the Colonial Military Expenditure. House of Commons, 1834.
Rey, HJM. *Essai sur le Topographie Médicale de Gibraltar et sur les Epidemies de Fievre Jaune qui ont Regné dans cette Place.* Paris, 1833.
Richardson, W. (ed. Childers, S) *A Mariner of England.* Murray, 1908.
Rochfort Scott, C. *Excursions in the Mountains of Ronda and Granada.* London, 1838.

Sawchuk, L.A. *Deadly Visitations in Dark Times.* Gibraltar Government Heritage Monographs No. 2. Gibraltar 2001,
Sawchuk, LA, and Benady, S. *Diary of an Epidemic: Yellow Fever in Gibraltar, 1828.* Gibraltar Government Heritage Publications, 2003.
Sepúlveda, I. *Gibraltar, la razón y la fuerza.* Alianza, 2004.
Steele, T. *Notes on the War in Spain.* London, 1824.
Shaw, A.G.L. *Sir George Arthur, Bart.* Melbourne University Press, 1980.
Stevens, J. *Victorian Voices.* Société Jersiaise, Jersey, 1969.
Sullivan, J. *General Sir George Don, Lieutenant Governor of Jersey.* Jersey, 1885.
Syuret, M. and Stevens, J. (editors) *Balleine's History of Jersey.* Phillimore, 1981.

Ticknor, G. *Life, Letters and Journals of George Ticknor.* Boston, 1876.
Traverso, AA. Dissertation. *A History of Education in Gibraltar.* University of Southampton, 1980.

Wylly. *History of the King's Own Yorkshire Light Infantry.*

158

INDEX

162

164